Oliver J. Thatcher

A Sketch of the History of the Apostolic Church

Oliver J. Thatcher
A Sketch of the History of the Apostolic Church
ISBN/EAN: 9783337403553
Printed in Europe, USA, Canada, Australia, Japan
Cover: Foto ©ninafisch / pixelio.de

More available books at **www.hansebooks.com**

A SKETCH OF THE HISTORY OF THE APOSTOLIC CHURCH

BY

OLIVER J. THATCHER
OF THE UNIVERSITY OF CHICAGO

BOSTON AND NEW YORK
HOUGHTON, MIFFLIN AND COMPANY
The Riverside Press, Cambridge
1893

TO MY TEACHER

PROF. ADOLF HARNACK

THE author wishes to express his thanks to his colleagues, Prof. ERNEST D. BURTON and Prof. NATH. BUTLER, Jr., for their kind criticisms and substantial help in preparing this book for publication.

CONTENTS.

CHAPTER	PAGE
I. The Condition of the World	1
II. The Expansion of Judaism	19
III. The Spread of Christianity	34
IV. The Church in Jerusalem during the First Fourteen Years	62
V. Breaking the Jewish Bonds	89
VI. The Burning Question	125
VII. The Best Years of Paul	159
VIII. The Last Years of Paul	254
IX. The Opposition to Christianity	273
X. Authorities, Government, and Worship	288
Conclusion	301
Appendix. The Chronology of the Period	307

A SKETCH OF THE HISTORY OF THE APOSTOLIC CHURCH.

CHAPTER I.

THE CONDITION OF THE WORLD.[1]

In the history of Christianity nothing is more remarkable than its rapid spread. Beginning as a Jewish sect whose founder had suffered the most shameful death, in an obscure province, among a people that had played no important part in the world's history and for many reasons was everywhere despised, it steadily advanced even in the face of fierce persecutions and obstacles of many kinds, until, within less than three hundred years from its first proclamation, it had so large and influential a following throughout the Roman world that the shrewd and calculating Emperor Constantine recognized that it could be made a most powerful support of his throne. And fifty years later the Emperor Gratian actually made it the only legal religion of the state. Besides this, it had spread beyond the now dwindling boundaries

---

[1] See also the great work by Friedlaender, *Sittengeschichte Roms*, on which this chapter is based.

of the empire, and the name of Christ was honored among barbarians and peoples that acknowledged no allegiance to Rome. And all this success without a stroke of the sword. Such a record has no parallel in history. It challenges our admiration, and demands an explanation.

How was this possible? "But when the fullness of the time came, God sent forth his Son." [1] That is Paul's answer to the question. In spite of the evil that is in the world, Paul believed that God was ruler. He was filled with the sublime thought that the God whom he served was the God who controlled men and nations. For Him no event could be a surprise, no result a disappointment. The history of the world was the history of the accomplishment of his purpose. The long delay in the coming of the promised Messiah was that the world might be made ready for Him. If we look at the condition of the world as it then was, we can easily understand what Paul meant by the "fullness of the time." Christianity made its appearance at the one time in the history of the world when all circumstances were most favorable for its spread. The time was ripe. The world was ready to receive, develop, and propagate such a faith.

If we look at the political condition of the world we are struck by the important fact that it was under the rule of one man. Rome, at first a city of husbandmen, had united under one sceptre all

[1] Gal. iv. 4.

her immediate neighbors. Her first successes led necessarily to other wars; for she had not only to defend her conquests, but also to make them secure from all danger of attack. The only way to accomplish this was to conquer the adjoining territory. She could make her frontier secure only by extending it. She was, therefore, logically forced into the career of a conqueror. She soon came to believe that it was her mission to rule the world. The *Orbis Romanus* was to be coterminous with the *Orbis terrarum*.

She had not been content to be mistress of the West alone, but had followed in the way of Alexander the Great to the East. For nearly a thousand years, beginning with his conquests, the Orient was forced to feel and unwillingly to confess the mental and military superiority of the Occident. This long period of western domination, of close contact and mutual influence, which was to be ended by the violent national reaction under Mohammed, was now reaching its acme. Communication between the East and the West had never before been so easy and unhindered. All the gates between them were open, the barriers gone. And in every khan and seaport crowds of Europeans with faces to the East jostled and elbowed the throngs of Asiatics and Africans that were in the great stream of travel to the West.

But there had just been made a most significant change in the form of government of this vast state. From a republic it had become an empire.

In theory it had two heads, the Emperor and the Senate; but in reality the Emperor was sole master. The power was in his hands, for he had the army. The Senate was powerless, and hence obsequious. As a matter of form the Emperor for a time consulted it, but it soon lost even the appearance of power, and became little more than an aristocratic club.

The early Christian apologists saw in this fact a mighty argument against Polytheism. They drew a parallel between the one Emperor who ruled the civilized world and the one God who ruled the universe. Even here on the earth it is necessary for the welfare of all that there be but one head, one will. How much more necessary for the harmony and the preservation of the universe that there be but one God to rule it? How else could the regular order of all things be preserved, the pleasant change of seasons, of night and day, the harmonious and regular movements of the sun, moon, and stars? The existence of many gods would make all this impossible. And when the Emperors began to associate with themselves their successors with the title of Cæsar, the further parallel was drawn between the Emperor and his crown prince, who was his helper, and God and his Son, to whom He had given a share in the government of the universe.

But this change in government had a deeper significance and more substantial effects in many ways. It meant that the world was indeed one land. The Roman armies had done their work well, and the national boundaries, which had been such hindrances to intercourse and progress, were wiped out. The once hostile nations were now peaceably passing through the same process; they were becoming Romanized. They were all on the road to Rome.

Great as Rome was in her conquests, she was even greater in her government. Of this, the province, which was her invention, was the peculiar characteristic. All the empire was divided into provinces, whose governors were responsible directly to the Senate, or to the Emperor. It was impossible that one uniform system of laws should everywhere be introduced at once. Roman laws, customs, and institutions could not replace those of the conquered in a day. The process of Romanizing was a slow and difficult one, but Rome had a genius for governing. She knew how much of her yoke a conquered people could bear. She knew how to control without oppressing too severely, and she was wise in subjecting them to influences which in the end would make faithful Roman subjects of those who had once feared and hated her.

The provincial governors had general directions to guide them in their difficult task. The size of the empire made it impossible for the Emperor to oversee everything in person, and the differences that still existed between the various parts of the empire prevented a rigidly uniform application of the laws. The peculiar circumstances in each province had to be regarded, and so it was imperative that the governors be allowed much liberty and independence of action. Sometimes they were little more than Roman police. But everywhere they had two objects in view: first, to keep the people quiet; and second, to Romanize them. They must make the best of everything, yield when necessary, and take advantage of every opportunity to advance the interests and increase the influence of Rome. Generally, they were left to their own judgment, and only in the more difficult cases did they appeal to the Emperor for instructions. From the nature of the case the legislation had to be special and local, not universal. The Emperors issued edicts for each province as the situation demanded. This lack of uniformity and fixedness in the laws and legislation was, in one respect, of great advantage to Christianity. It made a universal persecution almost impossible, because that must proceed from the Emperor in the form of an edict for the whole empire. The Christians might be persecuted in one province, while in all other parts of the empire they were undisturbed. The result of all this was that the Christian question was a local one until the middle of the third century. That is, there was no general edict against them until that time.

To add to the difficulties of the Emperor's position, the frontier was everywhere threatened by barbarians, and distant provinces were constantly revolting. So great and distracting were his duties that he could not have accurate knowledge of all that was going on in this vast territory. Through its organization the Church had become a great power, almost a state within a state, before the Emperors discovered that it was a menace to the existing order of things.

The influence of Rome on the conquered peoples was varied and profound. She set for herself the task of assimilating the world. All peoples must become Roman. No other nation has had such remarkable digestive and assimilative powers. She absorbed one after another of the conquered peoples, and of them all only one held fast to its nationality. The Jew remained a Jew, although a Roman. Her greatness awed and dazzled all and filled them with the desire of having a share in her glory. After coming into contact with Rome they lost in great measure their attachment to the little fatherland. They desired to be Roman, for to be Roman was to be a citizen of the world. To be anything else was to be provincial. Roman citizenship was for a long time the synonym of the highest and best that could be obtained. Her government was really a training-school for Roman citizenship. She tried to give all the world Roman laws, Roman culture, Roman modes of thought, Roman ideas. It was her aim to unify all peoples by Romanizing them, by lifting them up to her level. And so far had this process progressed that, in the year 215 A. D., Caracalla actually conferred the right of

Roman citizenship on all the inhabitants of the empire. To be sure, this right had lost much of its value then. It did not actually confer much, because what had been the peculiar possession and privilege of the Roman citizen was now the common property of all. That marks the progress which the world had made under the tutelage and government of Rome.

The change in the form of government hastened this process. The Emperor quickly replaced Rome in the thoughts and affections of the people. The homage that had once been Rome's was now his. He was a kind of personal as well as movable capital. Favors, privileges, and honors were in his hand. The way to fortune passed by his door. The bond of unity between the peoples and the Emperor was personal, and hence stronger than that between them and Rome.

But the Emperors did a still greater service. They brought peace with all its blessings to a world that was worn out with wars. The accession of Augustus marks the beginning of a new era of commerce and travel. The pirates who had infested the Mediterranean were driven from the sea, which was now covered by fleets of freight, passenger, and mail boats. By land, the many bands of brigands and robbers, while not entirely destroyed, were greatly checked in their depredations. Travelers then had little more to fear from these than the traveler of to-day in those parts; certainly much less than the traveler of fifty years ago. The Emperors made constant war on them, and stationed troops in all the dangerous parts of the empire for the protection of those who passed that way. They built magnificent roads, which covered the empire like a net. For state purposes, Augustus established a regular postal service throughout the empire. Wagons and horses for hire were everywhere to be had. Hotels, though not luxurious, and restaurants were to be found conveniently located along these roads. Commerce flourished, and people traveled as never before. We know of one merchant who made the sea voyage from Asia Minor to Rome seventy-two times. There was an immense amount of travel; everywhere one fell in with merchants and tradesmen, professors and students, tourists and pilgrims, physicians and quacks, painters and sculptors, actors, athletes, and musicians. The rich inhabitants of the cities sought the mountains or the sea in summer, and the sick went to the baths then as now.

The advantages of this state of things, which was brought about by the Emperors, are evident. In one word, *Christianity could travel.* The national barriers were gone. Roads led in all directions. There was a constant flux and flow of people to and from every quarter. Missionaries could go to all lands in safety. And under these circumstances Christianity could easily and quickly reach the utmost parts of the empire.

Of even greater significance is the fact that the world had a universal language. Greece surpassed all other nations in her literature and art, philosophy and science, industry and commerce; but one gift was denied her, the art of government. She never could unite her provinces under one government. The personal sense, the sense of individuality, and the desire to make this individuality felt by others, were so strong in her sons that they were incapable of harmonious action and could never be brought together into one great state. It was this characteristic that caused the supremacy in Europe to pass into the hands of the Romans. But Greece sent out numberless bands of colonists, and her merchants were in all the market-places in the world. Greek cities and communities sprang up in the midst of other peoples. Every city had a great number of Greek inhabitants, and commerce was largely controlled by them. They had taken their language with them, and at this time Greek was understood and spoken with more or less fluency from Spain to the valley of the Euphrates. Even in Rome, Greek was almost as much in use as Latin.

What a help for the missionary! Wherever he went, he would find those who could understand his message. It was not necessary that he first spend months, or perhaps years, in learning their language. The rapid evangelization of the world was possible because there was a universal language. How true this is can be seen in the fact that Greek became, as it were, the official language of Christianity. All the writings of the New Testament were composed in Greek, and for two hundred years all who wrote for the Christian public used the Greek, and not the Latin.

It would require a volume properly to describe the social condition of the Roman Empire. From one point of view there were three classes, the nobility, the people proper, and slaves. In the second class there were the greatest contrasts and extremes. The large majority were sunk in abject poverty. They had no influence, no possessions, no position, and no prospect of ever being treated as anything but ciphers by the great ones of this world. They could never hope to be recognized as individual human beings, with peculiar personal rights and dignity which made them the equal in worth, if not in worldly honor, of even the highest. The third class, the slaves, formed a large per cent of the whole population, and their condition was most wretched. They were wholly in the hands of their masters. They were mere chattels, not persons, and before the law they were without rights. It is hard for us to imagine with what joy such as these would receive the good news of a kingdom in which all should be brethren, and each should count one and only one, no matter what his birth or condition.

Two things had helped to develop an extensive club life among the people. First, the need of mutual help in times of distress, sickness, and death; and second, the innate desire of every one to be a member of some circle, however small, in which he has equal rights with all others. Christianity appealed to them in both ways, for it appeared to them as a brotherhood in which all were equal, and the words "mine" and "thine" meant the same thing, at least in all times of need.

It is natural to think that in those times there must have been great dearth of reading matter and little literary activity. But the names of the authors of the first century would make a long list. There was no printing-press, to be sure, but slaves did its work, and books were quickly and inexpensively made. Every publisher kept a large number of slaves who were trained penmen, and to these the work which was to be published was dictated. As one read, hundreds wrote; and when the reader had finished there were so many hundreds of copies ready to be put on the market. The book trade throughout the empire was large and important. There were many publishing houses, bookstores, and public libraries in the cities. In proportion there must have been as large a reading public then as now. The public libraries were visited by great numbers. New works by prominent authors were anxiously awaited, eagerly read, and quickly sent to the farthest provinces. Nor must we suppose that books were expensive. They were not so large as books now are, but many volumes were to be had at prices ranging from ten cents to one dollar, according to size and binding.

In philosophy it was a period of decadence in one respect, of progress in another. Of decadence, for the strict scientific method of the first philosophers was no longer in use. Close argumentation and reasoning had given way to fanciful allegorizing. They sought not valid proofs, not cause and effect, not essential characteristics, but fancied or accidental resemblances or differences. The progress consisted in this: philosophy had been speculative, it was becoming practical and religious. Instead of dealing with speculative problems, it was beginning to look upon morals and conduct as its proper field of inquiry and instruction. It was its business to tell people, not how to think, but how to live. Philosophy had once said, "You must *know* the truth;" she was now beginning to say, "You must *live* the truth." She was beginning to emphasize conduct instead of knowledge, the heart instead of the head. It was knowledge that had robbed death of its terrors for the older philosophers; now it was the consciousness of a well spent life, of duty done. We are in a period half way between Platonism, which was a philosophy, and Neo-Platonism, which was a religion. The change may be seen in this: *philosophy had at first meant speculation, it came to mean asceticism.* The real worth and dignity of man were seen to consist in his moral and religious character.

The religious and moral sense was improving. The age of Cicero was godless and sneering. The priests, conscious of the deceit they were practicing, exchanged knowing looks as they met in the streets. It was fashionable to laugh at the gods and make jokes about them. But an upward movement was beginning which was at the same time a reaction toward monotheism. A finer, higher conception of God and his relations to men was beginning to prevail, as is shown in the saying of Aratus quoted by Paul, Acts xvii. 28, "For we are also his offspring;" and in that of Epictetus, that God is the father of all men, and hence they are brothers, and brotherly love ought to prevail among them. These are the words of a heathen slave, but they contain the fundamental teaching of Christianity.

The progress in humanity, morals, and religion is further seen in the change of attitude toward slavery. Plato had not condemned it. Aristotle had thought it necessary, and in accordance with the natural order of things, that some should be slaves and be treated as property. But Seneca gave expression to the Christian thought that slaves, although socially beneath us, ought to be treated as our fellow-men, since before God, who is over all, we are their fellow-slaves. The immortality of the soul, although it could not be proven, was by many confidently believed, because the great Plato had taught it, and their instincts and feelings told them it was true. And Christianity, as the perfect ethical religion, with its confident affirmation of the existence of the one true, loving and forgiving God, and the promise of an endless life after death, appealed to this improved moral and religious sense with great power.

But let us look at some of the difficulties in the way of Christianity. In the first place, heathenism was the official religion of the empire. In the fullest sense of the word, Rome had a state religion, idolatrous practices of which were in the most intricate way woven into the web of everyday life. Every public or state transaction was at the same time a religious act, and had a fixed ritual or form, which in the eyes of all Christians must appear idolatrous. The Romans were in one sense of the word very religious. By every act they remembered their gods and offered a sacrifice, however small. With buying, selling, visiting, marrying, going to law, making a will, with births and deaths, with everything, in fact, there was connected some rite that would prevent Christians from participation. As citizens and neighbors, the Christians could perform neither their civil nor their social duties. It was this that so enraged the heathen, for it seemed to them that such conduct of the Christians could have but one result — the offended gods would send punishment on the whole land. The Christians were "atheists," because they despised the gods. And all public misfortunes, such as the failure of the crops, drouth, floods, pests, storms, earthquakes, and the like, were laid at their door; for all these were expressions of the anger of the gods. Hence persecutions were the necessary consequence.

Again, the Romans were hostile to Eastern religions. They tolerated them, indeed, in the East, but forbade their spread in the West. Judaism was the only exception. But Christianity was an Eastern religion. So long as it was regarded as a Jewish sect, it was tolerated; but when it became independent of Judaism and was seen to be making converts for itself and in its own name, it was in that very moment proscribed, and to be a Christian was in the eyes of the law to be a criminal.

Christianity met a powerful enemy in the new and universal religion that had just been invented. This was Emperor worship. In the days of the republic, the Romans had deified their city. According to Roman modes of thought, everything of value had a "genius" that presided over it. So temples were erected and sacrifices offered to the genius of Rome. When Augustus became Emperor, the same process of reasoning led them to deify him. To his Genius also temples were built, altars set up, sacrifices appointed, and a ritual fixed. His statues were everywhere, and to refuse to sacrifice before one of them was to be guilty of high treason, which was of course punishable with death. Christians were every day brought into contact with this practice, and as they had to refuse, persecution was the necessary result. This soon came to be the test in all trials of Christians. They were placed before a statue of the Emperor, and if they sacrificed they were set free; but if they refused, they were at once condemned to death.

Polytheism required only a ritual, not morals.

The dignity and glory of the gods consisted not in their *moral* character, and they made no moral demands of their worshipers. If the morals of the gods themselves would not bear close inspection, it was not to be expected that they would trouble themselves about the conduct of their worshipers. Worship did not imply any bond of moral union between the god and his worshiper. So it was customary to go to the temple of a god, to sacrifice, and to be initiated into his mysteries, and that was the end of it. The god could expect nothing more from his worshiper, and if he had anything to give, the worshiper had done all in his power to obtain it. Further connection between the two was not necessary. It naturally follows that there could be no bond of union, no "fellowship" among the worshipers; they were not gathered into congregations and bound together and to their god by bonds of love.

The worship of one god did not exclude that of others. On the contrary, if it was good to sacrifice to one god, it was twice as good to sacrifice to two. If one wished to be perfectly sure, one had to sacrifice to as many gods as possible. It was like taking out an insurance policy in many companies. And so, like Pausanias, the greatest religious tramp of the world, the people went from one temple to another, offering this external service, while their lives were uninfluenced. That the true God is jealous of the affections of his worshipers, that there must be a lasting union between Him and them, that they should be one with Him in will, love, and character, all this was foreign to their thoughts. And so there was great danger that the heathen would regard Jesus as another god to be added to their list, and would look on baptism and the Lord's Supper as the mysteries into which they must be initiated, and that that was all that could be required of them; that they would not understand that they had been made sons of God and brethren one of another, and that these new relations required a new manner of life. It was this that made it necessary for the author of the Hebrews to write, "not forsaking the assembling of ourselves together, as the custom of some is" (Heb. x. 25).

Further, it was an age of uncertainty and doubt in religion, and hence superstitious. The people listened to any one who claimed to be a messenger from the gods. That led to quackery in religion. There were false priests and prophets everywhere, making money by imposing on the credulity of the people by their tricks and deceptions. Christianity was sure to be abused and corrupted in the same way, for it offered a fine field for the operations of quacks and impostors, whose sole aim was gain and self glory.[1]

[1] Cf. Simon Magus, Acts viii.; Elymas, Acts xiii.; "strolling Jews," Acts xix.; *The Didache*, ch. xi.-xiii.; Lucian, Peregrinus Proteus.

CHAPTER II.

THE EXPANSION OF JUDAISM.[1]

From another quarter, the world received a preparation without which the great and rapid success of Christianity would have been impossible. Of all ancient religions, Judaism as represented by the Prophets was incomparably the best. No other religion had such a conception of God, his lofty and upright character, his majesty, his compassion, his fatherly love for men, his mercy, and at the same time, of the high demands for holy living which He made on all who would be his people and enjoy his protection. But this high conception of God was confined to one little people, inhabiting a small province and having little communication with the rest of the world. More than that, their foreign intercourse was so restricted by the many levitical rules and regulations that their religious influence on other nations was practically nothing. Everywhere else there was polytheism, varying in grade from its finest and noblest forms to the crassest, most degraded, and degrading. What advantage was it to the world that the Jews

[1] See also Schürer's work, *The History of the Jews in the Time of Christ.*

had a better religion, since the levitical law was a barrier that prevented all communication? It looked as if the heathen were to be excluded from having any share in the religious truth in which Israel was so rich. The heirs of the Prophets were by no means inclined to share their holy inheritance with the unclean heathen about them.

But there can be no lasting monopoly in truth. Deep and wide as was the gulf that separated the heathen from the Jews, it could be bridged. In spite of the separation, many means of contact and channels of communication could be found. This leads us to the study of one of the most interesting and important subjects, the Jews in the Diaspora.

Abraham, their great forefather, was himself a wanderer, and in this respect he had many imitators among his children. For centuries the Jews had been spreading beyond Palestine. A constant stream of emigrants was overflowing its boundaries in all directions. At this time there was scarcely a city in all the world that did not have Jews among its inhabitants. There were great numbers of them in the lands of the Tigris and Euphrates. Asia Minor was overrun by them. Alexandria in Egypt was divided into five districts or wards, two of which were occupied by the Jews. In the Nile Delta, it was estimated that there were more than a million Jews. Along the coast of North Africa they were everywhere at home. The towns and cities of Macedonia and Greece contained Jewish colonies. In Rome there were probably thirty thousand of them. The Jew was ubiquitous.

But in their wanderings and long residence in foreign lands they had undergone a most important change. If a paradox be allowed, they were not only Jews, they had also become Greeks, and consequently were neither Jews nor Greeks. They produced a new culture, a new civilization, composed of the best elements of Judaism and of Hellenism. The civilization of the Jews was in many respects very narrow and limited, but in others lofty and imposing. Its ideal was the knowledge and perfect observance of the law of God as contained in the Old Testament. It was monotheistic and intensely religious. The Greek civilization was far wider and more varied. It was great in science, literature, and art. Its type was not religious and moral, but intellectual and æsthetic. This new Hellenistic civilization was a union of the two. It got its religion from Judaism, its philosophy and its learning from the Greeks.

These Hellenistic Jews had no thought of becoming anything else than Jews. They were not sensible of any change. They did not feel that there was any difference between them and their brethren in Palestine. They kept up their connection with the Holy Land. Every year thousands of them made pilgrimages to Jerusalem, which still remained for them the holy city, the only place where they could acceptably offer sacrifice. They regularly sent their yearly contributions to the temple, and, whenever it was possible, they went in person to attend one of the yearly feasts. Besides this they took their law with them, and wherever they went, they met every Sabbath to study it. Wherever there were Jews, there was a synagogue. So by all these means they kept in touch with their brethren and the traditions of their fathers.

On the other hand, they lived among heathen, and were compelled to associate more or less intimately with them. They were brought into close daily contact with those who were their superiors in refinement and culture. The Jewish mind has always shown a good deal of alertness and receptivity. And it was impossible that they should remain insensible to all the beauties of the culture about them. Especially the fine speculations and teachings of the philosophers attracted them, for they seemed to be in harmony with their scriptures, and even, indeed, to express the same truths seen from a different point of view.

They held to the truth of their religion; they tried to keep the law, but it was impossible for them to remain Pharisees. They honored their father Abraham, and their lawgiver Moses. But they came into contact with people who had not Abraham for their father, and were ignorant of the law of Moses, and yet possessed much truth, were virtuous and upright, pursued noble ends, and lived blameless lives. A problem was thrust on them which they had to solve. Will these good people be excluded from the kingdom of God simply because they are not Jews? Their good sense in the end gave them the answer. It led them to distinguish between the truth, and the form in which the truth was expressed. Not the letter of the law was the important thing, but the religious and moral truth which it taught. To be a son of Abraham was a good thing, but truly to fear and honor God was far better. To observe the Mosaic distinctions of clean and unclean was important, but the necessary thing was to preserve a clean heart and live a pure life. In other words, here was a *liberal movement* among the Jews in the Diaspora which was entirely different from the Phariseeism of Palestine, and it need hardly be added, much superior to it; for it was a movement from the letter to the spirit, from the form to the content, from a religion of rites and ceremonies to a religion of the heart.

One of the most imposing things in Jewish literature is the unshaken confidence that they have the one true God, who will not tolerate the worship of anything else. They learned this with great difficulty, but they learned it well, and it has been to them a source of unlimited strength which centuries of persecution and oppression have not exhausted. While appreciating the good that existed among the heathen, they never ceased to abominate their idolatry. Their zeal for God led them to become missionaries to the heathen about them. We do not think of the Jews as a missionary people, but they have had a most interesting missionary period. For some centuries Judaism made earnest efforts to become a universal religion, to convert the world. But she was finally driven from the mission field by Christianity, which proved to be a too powerful rival; and at the same time Judaism drew back from the freer movement and settled down into a rigid, legal orthodoxy. In other words, Phariseeism prevailed over Hellenism.

The Judaism of Palestine was never attractive to the heathen, and hence was not a good missionary religion. To the heathen, many things in it were laughable, others offensive. Their refusal to eat swine's flesh led Juvenal to speak of Palestine as the land " where the long practiced clemency allowed the hogs to reach a ripe old age." They observed the Sabbath, it was said, because they were lazy and wished to shirk work. Since they had no statues in their temples or synagogues, they were charged with the foolishness of worshiping the clouds. Above all, the heathen were offended that the Jews assumed a superiority and refused to associate with them because they were levitically unclean. So for many reasons the Jews were despised and even hated.

It would seem, then, that the Jew could hope for little success in his missionary efforts. But it must be remembered that the Jews in the Diaspora were the real missionaries, and that they were already undergoing a radical change in their attitude to the ceremonial law. Consequently their desire to make converts led them to present only the most attractive features of Judaism to the consideration of their hearers. They took from the old Testament a few great ideas, *the essentials of their religion*, and laid all emphasis on these.

In the first place, they held strongly to the truth that there is but one God. They thereby introduced into the natural world, into history, and into religion, the principle of unity. The heathen thought of the world as the playground of malicious gods and spirits, which were lying in wait for an opportunity to play some mad prank in the realm of nature, cross the plans and purposes of some other god, or inflict an injury on some unsuspecting and helpless mortal. To the thoughtful heathen it was a great relief to learn that there is but one all-wise and powerful God, who has made and controls the universe.

And then, the lofty conception of God which they presented was attractive. He was so great and majestic, so high and spiritual, that it was an offense even to try to represent Him by anything material. No picture or statue was allowed; such things could only hinder and not help the mind in its attempt to conceive of Him and his greatness.

They made much of the doctrine of rewards and punishments in a future state. This God, so just and holy, is interested in his creatures, and will reward or punish each according to his life. The upright, the pure, and noble will receive at his hand the rewards for their conduct, while to the wicked will be meted out the just punishments for their disregard of his holy will.

One of the commonest and deepest feelings of the human heart is the sense of ill desert before God. The conscience is oppressed and burdened, and longs for some sure way of conciliating an offended God. The soul longs for certainty in religious matters. The current philosophy of the day was doing much to awaken and deepen this sense of sin. People felt their religious needs as never before. Of all ancient religions, Judaism offered the most satisfying symbolical rites and ceremonies of purification, and the most comforting assurances of the merciful and forgiving character of God. In one sense, these Jews in the Diaspora were the true successors of the Prophets, for like them they disregarded the letter of the law, and taught that a humble and penitent heart and a blameless, helpful life are what God requires.

Of the personal, individual labors of these missionaries, their conversations, arguments, exhortations, and pleadings, we know almost nothing, for they found no biographer. But of their burning zeal and far-reaching activity we can form a good estimate, if we look at their literary productions. They made use of every known form of literature to recommend Judaism and make its teachings known. For three centuries they produced a rich and varied missionary literature. It is impossible to describe this in detail, but we should at least take a brief review of its most important features.

It will serve the double purpose of showing their missionary zeal and the change which Greek influences had produced among them.

They translated the Old Testament from Hebrew into Greek. That was by no means simply for the benefit of the Jews themselves, they had the heathen also in view. Just as the Scriptures are now translated into various languages and used as means of advancing the missionary work, so the Old Testament was rendered into Greek that the heathen might more easily learn the religion of Israel. Some expressions that would be offensive to Greek taste and conceptions were omitted or altered, and various changes were made, all of which sprang out of one motive, the desire to make their religion more attractive to the heathen.

To further the same purpose, they wrote commentaries on the Scriptures, explaining them in accordance with the best teachings of the philosophers, and to please the Greek taste. They did not ask what the literal meaning of a passage is, but by the allegorical method of interpretation derived from it whatever teaching they desired. For instance, the story of the Creation was given in philosophical form. The command to abstain from swine's flesh, it was said, is not to be understood literally. God had not intended that it should be, but He had meant thereby to teach that they should not associate with those that are like swine, brutish and impure in character. In this way they got rid of all the troublesome commands in the ceremonial law, and at the same time made it appear to be a most wise and ingenious piece of legislation, an inexhaustible source of practical wisdom.

Closely akin to these commentaries were their philosophical works, inasmuch as these were often based on some section of Scripture, or at least treated the Old Testament as the source of all philosophy. The same allegorical method was used, and Moses and the Prophets were made to appear as the true philosophers, with whom Plato, Aristotle, and the others agreed in so far as these latter had uttered the truth. In this way the first place and the highest honors were vindicated to Judaism. These philosophical works all have this characteristic, which distinguishes them from the works of the Greek philosophers, namely: they all have a practical, moral, and religious object in view. The Greeks pursued knowledge for its own sake; the Jews, for the influence which it should have on the character and life. They made philosophy the handmaid of religion, for it was its function to make men better, to help them to a truly religious life.

The Jews were proud of their history. They believed that God's hand was visible in it all. Hence it was inevitable that they would use it too for missionary purposes. And so in fact we find that a great many histories of the Jews were written, in all of which there is a more or less pronounced Chauvinism. They all pursued the same end, the glorification of Israel. They all seek to show that the Jews have worshiped the true God, who has cared for them in the most remarkable way, and therefore they have played a great rôle in the history of the world. As a nation, they have a long and glorious past, because they stand in an intimate relation to the God of all the earth.

Epic poetry and the drama were also used to acquaint the heathen with Judaism, and to fill them with enthusiasm for Judæa's history and religion. As Homer had sung of Troy and her fate, so Philo, the epic poet, wrote the history of Jerusalem and her kings in the form of a great epic poem. Still more remarkable is the fact that the history of Israel was dramatized. Just as the Greek dramatists had chosen some great and decisive event in the history of their country for the subject of their greatest dramas, and thereby held up their history for the admiration of the world, so the Jews competed for praise and honor for their land by presenting its history in the same fascinating way. We have fragments of one of these plays, called "The Exodus," as its name indicates a dramatization of the biblical story of the Exodus from Egypt. Thus even the theatre was compelled to assist in the missionary work of the Jews.

But they found opponents who attacked them and made many severe charges against them. This shows that these missionary efforts were so strong and persistent that the heathen found it necessary to defend themselves and their religion, which they did by attacking the Jews. These attacks must be resisted, and so we find Jewish apologists writing in defense of their religion and people, and refuting at great length all the charges made against them. Two of these are especially worthy of notice. The Jews were charged with being a modern people, without a history, and consequently they had contributed nothing to the civilization of the world. To disprove these charges they put forth the most strenuous efforts. They sought for proofs from every quarter to show that they were as old as any of the peoples then existing. And they did not hesitate to declare that the Jews had been the source of *all* culture and civilization. Abraham had taught the Egyptians astrology; Joseph had introduced a new system of irrigation and agriculture; Moses was the real father of all learning, for he was the first great philosopher, had invented the alphabet, and written the Pentateuch, which was the greatest of all philosophical works. He had lived long before any of the great men of the Greeks, who had derived all their knowledge from him without giving him the proper credit.

Not content with all these efforts, they even made use of forgeries to increase the reputation and authority of their religion. The Sibyls were mysterious prophetesses that were held in great reverence by the heathen. It was very shrewd on the part of the Jewish missionaries to make use of the name of the Sibyl to propagate the Jewish faith, for anything that she might utter would at once receive the most ready credence. So in the second century B. C., we find that some pious Jew wrote a book which purported to be the work of a Sibyl. In the prologue she was made to say that she was a daughter of Noah, that she had been with him in the ark at the time of the flood, that she had then come from Babylon, and that the Greeks had given her a false name. She then foretells the glories of Solomon's kingdom, and really gives in the form of a prophecy the history of the Jews, Greeks, and Romans down to about the year 140 B. C. In all this the Jews are represented as the people of God, to whom is promised the Messiah, and all the other nations are threatened with destruction unless they repent and join the Jews in the worship of God. These prophecies of the Sibyls were widely read, and undoubtedly had great influence. Virgil and Tacitus had read them, and made use of them in their writings. Under the names of the greatest Greek poets and philosophers, Jewish writers also forged poems and histories, in which these are made to teach the purest Jewish doctrines and sound forth the praises of the true people of God.

This is certainly enough to show that the Jews were tremendously in earnest in their efforts to convert the world. Such a varied and eager missionary activity will compare favorably with that of any other religion. They bid high for popular favor, and left no stone unturned to reach the heathen masses. Their efforts were not without success. The influence of the Jews on the heathen world was far greater than has generally been supposed. Many heathen became proselytes. They were circumcised, observed the whole law, and lived entirely as Jews. These were called "proselytes of righteousness." A far larger number, however, were influenced by their religious teachings, yet hesitated to take this important step. They were willing to observe some of the law, but in its entirety it was too exacting and burdensome. Many of these observed the Sabbath and some of the requirements in regard to meats, and with this the Jews seem to have been satisfied. These were called "God fearing" or "devout."[1]

There were also many that were influenced by the teachings of the Jews, although they refused to accept any of these burdensome and inconvenient restrictions. They learned much from the Jews. We might even say they got the true religion from them. They were careful to receive the truth and to frame their lives in accordance with it. But the ceremonial part of Judaism was repellent to them, and, furthermore, they saw that it was not necessary.

From what has been said it will be seen that the influence of the Jews on the heathen was great and good, converting many of them wholly to a

---

[1] These and similar phrases were used to designate this class. Thus Cornelius, Acts x. 2, is called a "devout man and one that feared God." Cf. Acts xiii. 50, "the devout women;" xvi. 14, "one that feared God." These were not called "proselytes of the gate;" this phrase was applied simply to heathen who lived in Palestine.

high type of Judaism, and giving many others a better knowledge of God and of his character. Every synagogue was as a light set in a dark place, and about each of these were gathered many heathen seeking the truth, and worshiping with more or less purity the God of Israel. The scattering of the Jews throughout all lands was in this way a blessing; for they were instrumental in spreading abroad a higher conception of God and purer moral standards, thus helping on the religious education and development of the world, and preparing it for the reception of Christianity.

CHAPTER III.

THE SPREAD OF CHRISTIANITY.

WHATEVER the purpose of the author of the so-called "Acts of the Apostles" was, it may be regarded as a sketch of the first thirty years of Christian missions. If that really was the author's aim, he did not follow it closely, and has consequently failed to tell us many things that we would wish to know. He has given us a good deal of information and many hints about the spread of Christianity, which we may put together, but still we shall be far from knowing all about it. It is impossible, indeed, to answer all the questions that present themselves, because our sources of information are so meagre.

In general, we know that for some years Christianity appeared very much as a Jewish sect, confined strictly to the Jews. Its followers had no thought of leaving the Jewish fold, but rather expected that all the Gentiles should become Jews in order to have a part in the Messiah's kingdom which they were establishing. But Christianity was stronger than its followers. It had such expansive power that it was not to be hemmed in. And so in spite of its adherents it broke off the fetters of the ceremonial law, freed itself from all that was peculiarly national, and asserted its independence. Greek Jews preached the new gospel to heathen who accepted it as something complete in itself, needing nothing from Judaism and the ceremonial law. A Christian society was formed in Antioch, in which heathen and Jew associated as brethren, apparently without ceremonial distinctions. From this time, Christianity spread rapidly under two forms. The one, Jewish Christianity, in which circumcision and the observance of some parts of the law were required of the heathen; the other, after the model of the church at Antioch, free from all legal observances and distinctions. It spread with amazing rapidity throughout Palestine and the neighboring countries of Asia Minor. By the year 50, it was in Rome. Before 60, it was said in popular hyperbole to be preached all over the inhabited world. Before 100, it was well established in almost all the principal cities of the Empire, had attracted the attention of Emperors and their governors, had endured sharp local persecutions, and was rapidly increasing its already large and enthusiastic following.

Here is more than a half century of magnificently successful mission work. But what do we know about the missionaries and the details of their work? Unfortunately, very little. The records of it are very scant. There were no Boards to control the work, send out missionaries, publish reports, open up new stations, make great plans, and appeal for money to carry on the work. There were no Missionary Journals, and no societies that were proud to publish the record of their successes. No one wrote the biography of the missionaries, or compiled the history of the missions. We have not even a list of the names of the missionaries. It was for us, for the most part, a nameless multitude that went everywhere preaching Jesus and his resurrection.

Let us follow out the various lines as indicated in the Acts, and in the Epistles which contain anything that bears on this subject. According to the Acts, the Twelve are represented as spending several years preaching and teaching in Jerusalem. Even when the persecution came, it was only the brethren that were scattered: in some way unknown to us, the Twelve were able to remain there. Strange as it may seem, for eight or ten years they seem to have confined their personal labors wholly to Jerusalem. Here they would meet the multitudes that came to the feasts, and in so great a city they would probably have ample opportunity for mission work. And yet, if Christ had told them to go into all the world and preach the gospel to every creature, to make disciples of all the nations, their conduct must seem somewhat strange. Since they remained so long in the Jewish capital, and confined themselves to working among the Jews, they must still have thought of the Messiah's kingdom as Jewish, and its success dependent, first of all, on the recognition of the messianic claims of

Jesus by the whole nation. This kingdom was to them still a political, national one. It is morally certain that Christianity had gone beyond the walls of Jerusalem. That, however, was not brought about by the efforts of the Twelve, but rather by those who had come to some feast and had gone away believing in Jesus, and carrying the news of the Messiah to those who, less fortunate than themselves, had not been able to go to Jerusalem.

The first notice of any preaching outside of Jerusalem is given in connection with the death of Stephen. A persecution arose and "They were all scattered abroad throughout the regions of Judæa and Samaria," "and went about preaching the word" (Acts viii. 1-4). The persecution which was intended to destroy the heresy only helped to spread it more widely and rapidly. Driven from their homes, they seem to have gone forth joyfully, finding consolation in the message which they carried. Some of them seem to have devoted themselves wholly to this mission work. It is difficult for us to appreciate the greatness of this. It is always easier to follow where others have gone before and marked out the way, than to strike out a new path for ourselves. How great must have been the impulse from within, how strong the consciousness of the possession of truth, to push these men and women out as pioneers in the work of spreading the good news of the Messiah! They traveled as far as the island of Cyprus, and into the land of Phœnicia, and reached Antioch. From Acts ix. 19

and 31, we learn incidentally that there were Christians in Damascus, and in Judæa, Galilee, and Samaria; but nothing is said about how the gospel was brought to them. Like most of the mission work of this whole period, it is, for us, anonymous. We know almost none of the details of the founding of churches in those parts. We have a short sketch of Philip's labors, which may perhaps serve as a sample of the work done, but this by no means covers the whole ground.

Two things about this work must be noted, for they are of the utmost importance in forming a correct idea of Christianity as it was understood by its earliest adherents, and especially by the Twelve. The first of these is that this work was done by the rank and file of the believers. The Twelve did not even lead in it. There is no indication that they had anything whatever to do with it. How far they were influenced by the idea of a kingdom with Jerusalem as its capital in which they were to be the men of honor and power, it is now impossible to say. But it is certainly significant that they all remained so long in Jerusalem, which as the Jewish capital must of course become the capital of the new kingdom. They seem after a while to have gone out to oversee and pass judgment on the work done by others, but it is not until long after the others had broken the way and had met with unexpected and extraordinary success that we find the Twelve following the same method.

The second thing is, that the gospel for so long a time was preached *only to Jews*. They seem not to have thought it possible to separate Christianity from Judaism, the gospel from Jewish forms. They preached a Jewish Messiah, and for the Jews. They had no message for the heathen, except as they should become Jews by accepting the law with all its obligations. Everything goes to show that they regarded themselves simply as Jews who believed that Jesus was the Messiah. They might properly be called a Jewish sect.

Then come indications of a change. We have a transition period, in which Christianity seems to be feeling its way out into the world. It was a period in which there was some sporadic mission work among the heathen; this, however, met with opposition from the Christians in Jerusalem. The old bottles were to them just as valuable as the new wine, for without them it seemed that the wine could not possibly exist.

This sporadic work among the heathen began in various places and probably about the same time, but again we know very little about the details. Of the beginning made by Paul, we know only that the call came to him in or near Damascus, that he obeyed at once, and went into Arabia, and then back to Damascus, and soon afterwards to Cilicia. That, however, is absolutely all that we know.

We have a long account of how Peter was brought to preach to Cornelius, who was still a heathen, although he feared God. He was one of those who had been brought into contact with Judaism, had taken its teachings without its forms, and hence is called a "devout" man. This was at least eight or ten years after the crucifixion, and yet Peter was the first of the Twelve to be brought into connection with the heathen. One has only to read this account in order to see how thoroughly Jewish they still were. The heathen were for them the common and unclean, with whom they could have absolutely no association. Peter was still so far from understanding the real character of the gospel that it required a great deal of supernatural machinery to bring him to preach to a heathen. He himself was surprised at the result of his preaching. The same extraordinary manifestations occurred here in the case of the heathen as had already taken place among the Jewish Christians. They received the Holy Spirit. But the Christians at Jerusalem were by no means pleased with Peter's conduct, for when he returned they rebuked him sharply for having associated with the uncircumcised. And it was only when Peter had told them the whole story, and showed them that God had made no difference between them and the Jews who believed, that they were quieted. We shall see that they were silenced by his arguments, but not convinced.

We have a brief account of another beginning that was made among the heathen. Peter seems to have gone no further along the new line of work opened before him in so mysterious a way. His

Jewish surroundings were too strong for him, and he drew back and remained the Apostle of the circumcision. If the mission to the Gentiles had depended on the Twelve, the Gentiles would have waited long and perhaps in vain. The honor of carrying them the gospel must be awarded to others, and not to the Twelve. According to Acts xi. 19–21, it belongs to some men of Cyprus and Cyrene, who had taken up the mission work in earnest. These, after traveling through Phœnicia and Cyprus, had come to Antioch, but preaching only to Jews. The important change was made in Antioch, for it was here that they began to preach also to the Greeks. They met with great and unexpected success, for many believed and turned to the Lord. Under the influence of a fresh enthusiasm, born of the consciousness of great and new spiritual possessions, Jews and Greeks united here and associated as brethren. Ceremonial distinctions were forgotten, they seem to have fallen away of themselves. It is difficult for us to realize what a revolution that was. How powerfully Christianity must have taken hold of the hearts of these Jews, since they were able to break, at once and without pain, with all the strongest and dearest traditions of their lives.

The church at Jerusalem, it is said, heard of this, and sent Barnabas down to Antioch to see what they were doing. He understood the situation at once. He saw that Christianity among the heathen was a success. He recognized that in that great city there was a fine field for work, and that there was need of an able man to carry it on. So he went to Tarsus to fetch Paul, who had now for some years been working there. Undoubtedly Barnabas knew of his work and felt that he was the man for the place. From this time on we have Paul as the most able representative and defender of this mission work among the heathen. The truth is proclaimed that the gospel is for all who believe in Jesus as the Messiah.

Again it must be noted that this was probably ten or twelve years after the death of Jesus. In all this time only one of the Twelve had come into contact with the heathen, and he had been opposed by some of the Christians at Jerusalem. In these twelve years there had been no spontaneous movement on the part of the Twelve and of the mother church at Jerusalem toward the heathen. They had not comprehended Christianity in its freedom and universality. They were not at all committed to the universal proclamation of the gospel. "Laymen" had begun the work among the heathen, the Twelve had only reluctantly followed. They had not inaugurated the new movement.

Every idea that is to become universal and overcome all opposition must have a leader who will in a sense be its personification. In him it will come to its full self-consciousness. He will give it a fixed form and the best statement possible. Such a leader must be a man of genius, of broad culture, and of consecration. He must make it the one work of his life to bring all the world to accept his truth. And that is what Paul was to this new and liberal movement in Christianity. He was the embodiment of the idea of the universalism and freedom of the gospel. He saw that it was for all, both Jew and Gentile, regardless of race or ritual. He perceived that Judaism had done its work, and was now superseded by something higher and better.

Like all new and liberal movements, this was sure to be opposed. Hence it had to have a home. It could not live "in the air." It needed a stronghold, a place where it could establish and develop itself independently of all opposition. It must have a kind of headquarters for carrying on the work of propagating itself. And this is what Antioch was to the young Gentile Christian church. Over against the mother church at Jerusalem, whose members were now and for many years to come "zealous for the law," we have another mother church of the Gentile Christians at Antioch. It was planted by laymen, and trained by Paul and Barnabas. The character of its teachers, its rapid growth, its location in a great and busy city, and its distance from Jerusalem, all made it impossible for the Jewish mother church to control its development. Some of the most important questions that arose in the early church were first agitated and settled in this congregation.

Antioch was the third city in size and importance

in the world. It was cosmopolitan in character. It had great wealth, and was noted for its commerce, schools, literature, and general culture. It was there that Christianity really made its first bow before the heathen public and entered as a great fact and factor on the stage of the world's development and civilization. By establishing itself in Antioch, Christianity challenged the attention of all classes, and it had there far wider opportunities than at Jerusalem. It was there that Christianity really broke with Judaism and came to its full self-consciousness. It was no longer a part of Judaism, a kind of appendage or complement to it, but separate and independent. "The disciples were called Christians first in Antioch" (Acts xi. 26). The people saw that they were not merely a Jewish sect. "Christian" was probably a nickname, but it was a good one, for it indicated the position which Jesus occupied in their thought and speech. Their distinguishing characteristic was that they believed that Jesus was the Christ.

Antioch became the centre of a great missionary activity. Until about 51, Paul seems to have been connected more or less closely with this congregation, beginning and ending his missionary travels there. According to Acts xiii. 1 ff., Antioch may be regarded as the home of foreign missions, for it was here that they received their first great impulse. Conscious of itself, its powers, and its purpose, Christianity began its conquest of the world at Antioch. From this time on, there is systematic evangelization of the heathen. The principle is recognized that the gospel of Jesus needs nothing from Judaism to make it complete. The door into the Messiah's kingdom is open to all, and it is not necessary to pass through Judaism to reach it. The law had been but the preparation for Christianity. It was not of itself holy. It had done its work, and hence was no longer binding.

That seems to us a very simple truth, but it was a staggering and incomprehensible doctrine to the Jews and Jewish Christians. When we remember that they were brought up to regard the law and the temple as the most holy objects on earth, we are not surprised that they refused to listen to it. For them, Christianity was but the complement of Judaism. They could not believe that Christianity was to displace it. So from this time, we have two lines of missionary work, — the one, Jewish Christian, confining itself largely to the Jews, or at least requiring the heathen to observe a part of the Mosaic law; the other, entirely free from all such burdensome requirements; Jews and Gentiles meeting together on an equal footing, and regarding each other as brethren and fellow-citizens in the new kingdom of God.

Of this Jewish Christian mission work, we know very little except that it existed. Up to the year 51, Peter had undoubtedly been working along this line; for in Gal. ii. 7, Paul says that the "pillars" in the church at Jerusalem recognized that Paul had been intrusted with the gospel to the

Gentiles, *as Peter with that to the Jews.* But when we ask where Peter had labored and with what success, we get for an answer only a few vague notices of his work. From Acts ix. 32 ff., we learn that " as Peter went throughout all parts " he came to Lydda and Joppa, and from there went to Cæsarea. And we find him very soon again in Jerusalem, whence he was compelled to go " to another place," because of the persecution of Herod (Acts xii. 17). This was in the year 44. Six years later he was again in Jerusalem. Soon after we learn that he was in Antioch, where he began to associate with the Gentile Christians. From this time he seems to have entered a wider mission field and to have traveled as a missionary among the heathen, imitating Paul and Barnabas.

In relating the agreement that was made between the " pillar " apostles and himself and Barnabas, Paul says that James and Peter and John gave them the right hand of fellowship that " we should go unto the Gentiles and they unto the circumcision." That implies that John and James also engaged in this mission work, but we have not the slightest notice of their travels.

In speaking of his meeting with the apostles at Jerusalem in the year 50 or 51, Paul mentions only Peter and John of the Twelve. James the brother of John was already dead, having suffered martyrdom in the year 44. But where were the other nine? We have not the slightest information about them. We can only say that it is probable that they were engaged in work, perhaps in Palestine, or among the Jews in the East, or Paul may have mentioned only the three that were the most prominent. They may, indeed, have been in Jerusalem at that time, but it is more probable that they were not. From 1 Cor. ix. 5 we may certainly infer that at least some of the disciples as well as some of the brothers of Jesus were at that time (about 56 or 57) traveling as missionaries, but still there is no hint as to where they were. That this mission had been very successful we learn from Acts xxi. 20, where it is said that thousands of the Jews believed, and that they were all still zealous for the law. It is clear, then, that this type of Christianity actually spread among the Jews in Palestine and perhaps in the East, but we are left without much definite information about it.

We get more light from Paul's letters to the Galatians and to the Corinthians. From these we learn that at least one branch of these Jewish Christians had entered the field as determined and outspoken opponents of Paul and the free gospel which he was preaching. They had begun to undo his work by carrying on a most vigorous propagation of the law in the free Gentile congregations which he had founded. At first, they met with success, but Paul vigorously defended himself and his doctrine, and in the end was victorious.

We are much better informed about a part of the work among the Gentiles, but even here we get only glimpses of the work and of the workers;

for of all that engaged in this, only one group is well known. The head and leader of this was Paul. He gathered about him a large number of young missionaries who worked with him and for him, serving him as special messengers and helpers. By means of these he kept in touch with his various congregations, and through their labors he became the spiritual father of many other churches, for they all followed his principles and preached his gospel. A long list of these might be made. There were Timothy and Titus, Erastus and Silas, Sopater, Aristarchus, Secundus and Gaius, Tychicus and Trophimus. Luke and Mark were with him at least a part of the time. In all his letters, we find others mentioned incidentally in such a way as to show that they were also engaged with him in the work.

Aquila and Priscilla also formed a part of this circle of Paul's friends and helpers, at least for a time. They labored with him in Corinth and in Ephesus, but afterwards returned to Rome where they continued the work, although independently of Paul.

In this connection the last chapter of the Epistle to the Romans [1] is exceedingly interesting, for it

[1] Many learned men think that the 16th chapter of Romans does not really form a part of the original letter, but is rather a letter of introduction for Phœbe to the church at Ephesus. In support of this, they call attention to the fact that the last verse of the 15th chapter really forms a very appropriate ending for the letter. Besides this, there are several things in the 16th chapter that seem to point to the church at Ephesus rather than to that of Rome. For instance, Aquila and Priscilla had recently

gives us a most surprising hint of the remarkable activity of these early missionaries. In this chapter Paul greets by name more than twenty persons, most of whom he seems to have known personally. If this be the case, he must have made their acquaintance in the East, for at this time Paul had not been in Rome. Several of these seem to have been connected with him in the work, and were united to him by the closest ties of friendship. Not only the common faith, but also fellowship in work and danger had bound them together. Some of them he greets as independent missionaries and evangelists who were traveling and laboring in the interests of the gospel. This chapter, then, gives us a most interesting glimpse of the missionary activity and travel of the period, since it shows that so many of those that had been in the East were now in Rome. For it is not to be supposed that we have here the names of all that were engaged in this work. In fact, we know that these were by no means all the workers. We learn of others who labored entirely independently of Paul and his company, although they seem to have fol-

been in Ephesus, and there is no hint anywhere else that they had returned to Rome. Epænetus is called "the first fruits of Asia unto Christ." Then they say that it is impossible that Paul should have known so many people in a city in which he had never been. That, however, is easily explained if the letter were addressed to the church at Ephesus where Paul had just spent three years. But Lightfoot has most ably refuted these arguments and shown that there is really nothing in the way of accepting this as a part of the original letter written by Paul to the Romans.

lowed his principles rather than those of the Jewish Christians. Apollos, a learned Jew from Alexandria, at least as early as the year 54 began this wandering missionary life, but not as a member of Paul's party. We find him first at Ephesus. From the brethren there he received letters of introduction to the brethren in Achaia, and he must have spent some time in Corinth. But when Paul wrote the first letter to the Corinthians he was again in Asia. Unfortunately, it is impossible to follow him further, for we have no later account of him.

Barnabas is said to have gone with Paul on the journey to Cyprus, and to the interior of Asia Minor, an account of which is given in Acts xiii.-xiv. But afterwards he and Paul were separated, and each went his own way. From the language of Paul in 1 Corinthians ix. 5, we are justified in inferring that Barnabas was still, that is about the year 56 or 57, traveling as an apostle among the heathen, but of his work and success we know absolutely nothing.

Again, in Romans xvi. there are several persons mentioned who seem to have been well known as missionaries or apostles, but who had not in any way been dependent on the leading or example of Paul. He speaks of Andronicus and Junias, his kinsmen, who because of their labors were noted apostles, and if they had not preceded Paul in the work, they had at least been earlier brought to believe in the Messiahship of Jesus. It is not at all improbable that the group of persons named in the fourteenth verse formed a band of missionaries that traveled together. And Apelles, in verse 10, is spoken of as one whose standing is secure because of his successful labors. When we consider that we have so few writings that serve us as sources of information about this period, we conclude that there must have been many others who are entirely unknown to us, for Christianity spread rapidly and we find it established in many places without being able to tell how it was brought thither. This activity was so great as to fill the heathen with wonder. The impression which it was making on them is expressed most graphically in the words of the leaders of the mob in Thessalonica. "*These that have turned the world upside down are come hither also*" (Acts xvii. 6).

Christianity was early established in Rome. The only notice we have of its introduction there is in the work of a heathen writer. Suetonius, in his "Life of the Emperor Claudius," chapter xxv., says that the Emperor expelled the Jews from Rome some time between the years 48 and 51 A. D., because of riotous disturbances among them which were stirred up by one *Chrestus*. It is generally conceded now that this has reference to the introduction of Christianity among the Jews there. We know from other sources that for two centuries or more the name of Christ was commonly mispronounced Chrestus by the common people and the Christians were called Chrestians. Suetonius was a heathen who had not come into direct contact with these troubles among the Jews, but was dependent on others for his information. Being ignorant of the exact details, he supposed that Chrestus was the real leader of the riots, and not the one about whom the contention was. From this passage, then, it is probable that Christianity had already made a beginning in Rome. Some of the Jews believed and were laboring for the conversion of others. But as in so many other places, this met with opposition which led to violent and riotous demonstrations, and the Emperor forbade the meeting of the Jews, thinking that thereby the difficulty would be overcome. It is not strictly true that the Emperor banished the Jews from Rome. He seems rather to have forbidden their meetings, which, in its practical effects, was equivalent to expelling them. This edict, however, was not long enforced. The Jews were disturbed by it only for a short time.

When Paul landed as a prisoner in the spring of 61 at Puteoli (now Pozzuoli, near Naples), he found Christians there with whom he spent a week. We have no knowledge of how long this congregation had been in existence or who had founded it.

Curious and interesting, too, is an inscription which was found on the wall of a house in Pompeii in the course of the excavations there, only a part of which could be read. The gentlemen engaged in the work of excavation declared that the letters HRISTIAN could be made out, but all that preceded or followed was too indistinct to be read. It seems that the only letters that could be supplied would be C at the beginning and U S or I at the end. If that be true, it would certainly be some reference to the Christians, and we would be justified in supposing that there were Christians in Pompeii at the time of its destruction in the year 79 A. D. But others have questioned the correctness of those who first read the inscription, and claim that it should be read in a different way. Unfortunately, the letters soon faded after being exposed to the light, and hence we now have no means of determining just what they were.

The Jews in the Diaspora were a very important factor in the spread of Christianity. They had not only prepared the soil, they now helped to sow the seed. As has been said they were everywhere, and the Roman empire was covered with a network of synagogues which, by means of the numerous pilgrims, were in constant communication with Jerusalem. Anything that deeply disturbed or agitated Jerusalem would surely and quickly be felt in the farthest Jewish communities throughout the empire. And so when Christianity came, it spread along these lines of Jewish travel as fire by a fuse. Many a Jew heard of Christ and believed on him while at Jerusalem as had the "men of Cyprus and Cyrene" (Acts xi. 20), and, like them, returned preaching the gospel in the synagogues by the way. The service which these synagogues rendered in the spread of Christianity is incalculable. It was not necessary for such a missionary to make any efforts to secure a place of meeting and then to get an audience together. These were already at hand in the synagogue. Every Sabbath he was sure to find there a band of Jews and proselytes, of devout and inquiring heathen, gathered together for religious instruction. In these services, strangers were generally invited to speak, and so he would, without any difficulty, obtain an opportunity of telling his message.

It would be interesting to know what classes were reached and won by these restless and eager missionaries. We can answer the question only in a general way. It would seem from all the scattered indications that the majority of the converts were from the lower and poorer classes. This is also in itself very probable, for these classes were by far the most numerous. The upper classes, the wealthy, the learned and literary, seem not to have taken any notice of Christianity until in the second century. Perhaps the congregation at Corinth was a typical one in its make-up, and its general character at least is indicated in the words of Paul: "For behold your calling, brethren, how that not many wise after the flesh, not many mighty, not many noble" (1 Corinthians i. 26). There must have been many slaves among the first converts, for in almost every letter there is some special advice given them. They are admonished, warned, or comforted in such a way as to make us infer that they formed a large part of the various congregations. And yet this is not to be pressed too far, for there were many that were masters, and some that had houses which could serve as meeting places for the Christians. There were some that were able to practice hospitality, whose doors were open to all the Christians who passed their way. There were some that were able to contribute largely to the funds that were to be sent to the poor in Jerusalem.

Again, in regard to this, we may see the beneficial influence of the Jews in the Diaspora, in preparing the way for the gospel. Through their missionary efforts many heathen had been made acquainted with the principal truths of the Old Testament. As all these were more or less closely connected with the synagogues, they were the first to hear the gospel. We have many indications of the deep joy with which these heard and received the gospel, for it offered them more than Judaism could give them and without any of the burdensome regulations which hampered them in Judaism. Undoubtedly, most of the converts to Christianity for many years had already been under the influence of Judaism. Decisive proof of this is found in all Paul's letters, for although they were addressed to those that had been heathen, they all presuppose a considerable knowledge of the principles and teachings of the Old Testament. It is also confirmed by many notices in the Acts of the glad and ready reception of the gospel by the proselytes and the devout Greeks. "Herein is the saying true, one soweth and another reapeth. I sent you to reap that whereon ye have not labored: others have labored and ye are entered into their labors" (John iv. 37 f.).

Since, in general, our information is so scanty, it will be worth our while to look more closely at some of the incidental notices which we have. From Paul's letter to the Philippians, i. 13, written about the year 62, we learn that Paul had made converts among the soldiers that guarded him. The prætorian guard was a part of the garrison of Rome, consisting of about ten thousand men, and to these Paul had been intrusted for safe keeping. Paul's language is somewhat rhetorical and hyperbolical, and it would be rash to attempt to make any estimate of the number of those who had become Christians. So much is clear, however; Paul had made use of the opportunities offered him and had preached Christ to the various soldiers that guarded him, so that even his captivity had resulted in the progress of the gospel.

At the end of this same letter we have one of those peculiarly interesting salutations: "All the saints salute you, especially they that are of Cæsar's household." Is it possible that some members of the family of the Emperor Nero were Christians? The language used seems not to allow any other interpretation. But the word "household" has a wider meaning when applied to a Roman family, for it includes also all the slaves, freedmen.

hangers-on, and officers, as well as the blood relatives. If we combine this passage with Romans xvi. 10, 11, we are able to find out something more about the members of the household of Cæsar who were Christians: " Salute them that are of the household of Aristobulus. Salute Herodion my kinsman. Salute them of the household of Narcissus which are in the Lord." The form of the salutation indicates that Aristobulus and Narcissus belonged to the wealthier class, and we are interested to know whether we have any other source of information about them. It is not said here that they themselves were Christians, but only some members of their households.

But who were Aristobulus and Narcissus? Strangely enough, heathen writers tell us about an Aristobulus and Narcissus who were famous in Rome at this time. Tacitus (Annals, xi. 29 ff.; xii. 57; xiii. 1) tells us that Narcissus, once a slave of the Emperor Claudius, had been set free and served his former master in the capacity of private secretary. He is said to have had great influence over the Emperor. He had made use of his position to amass great wealth, and was one of the most important and influential men in Rome. Aristobulus was a grandson of Herod the Great, who lived mostly in Rome. He too possessed great influence, because of his friendships and his immense wealth. From the fact that Paul greets his " kinsman Herodion " in direct connection with the household of Aristobulus, it is not at all improbable that this Herodion was a member of his family. At the time that Paul wrote this letter, it is probable that they were both dead, but their slaves had passed into the hands of the Emperor Nero, and it was customary for such persons still to bear the name of their former master.

From another source we know also the names of two more members of this congregation at Rome who also belonged to Cæsar's household. About the year 95, the peace of the congregation at Corinth was greatly disturbed by internal disputes and strifes. In consequence of this, the congregation at Rome wrote a letter to the church at Corinth, and at the same time sent two old men who had been Christians "from their youth up," men of upright character and approved wisdom, who should endeavor to settle the difficulties in Corinth and restore peace. Their names are also given in the letter as Claudius Ephebus and Valerius Bito. The name Claudius most certainly shows that Ephebus had been the slave of the Emperor Claudius, and as Valerius was the family name of his wife, Messalina, Bito had as certainly been her slave. Since they were now old men and had been Christians from their youth up, they had certainly seen Paul, and were members of the congregation at the time that Paul wrote his famous letter to the Romans. If only one of these had seen fit to write his own biography, how thankful we should have been to him!

These all belonged to the family of the Emperor,

but they were only slaves. Did Christianity go no higher in the social scale in the court at Rome? Or were there Christians among the nobility, or perhaps even in the very family of Nero himself? Again we are indebted to Tacitus (Annals, xiii. 32) for a bit of interesting information. The wife of the great Roman General Plautius, who conquered Britain, was named Pomponia Græcina. About 57 or 58 A. D. she was charged with being a convert to a foreign superstition. According to the Roman custom, her husband was ordered to try her on this charge. We have no account of the trial, but we are told that her husband pronounced her innocent. How much influence his heart exercised on his judgment we cannot tell, but probably it had much to do with her exculpation. For in spite of the fact that she was declared innocent, the historian further tells us that the lady lived in retirement for about forty years after this, wholly given up to a gloomy religion. He does not call her a Christian, but his language is very like that used in describing Christians, who were compelled to live in retirement, shunning all society, because they did not wish to expose themselves to censure. They could not take any part in public life without either engaging in idolatrous practices, or, by refusing to do so, subjecting themselves to criticism and persecution. Certain it is, at any rate, that some of her slaves were Christians, for their burial places have been discovered in the Christian Catacombs of Rome.

But Christianity came still nearer to the throne of the Cæsars. About the year 95, the Emperor Domitian put to death his cousin, the Consul Titus Flavius Clemens, on the charges of a "contemptible inactivity" and of "atheism." His wife, Flavia Domitilla, was at the same time and for the same reasons banished to an island in the Mediterranean. This Domitilla was, beyond all peradventure, a Christian. Her name is inseparably connected with the early history of the church at Rome. One of the many Catacombs in the neighborhood of Rome bears her name, and contains the graves of many of her slaves and followers who also became Christians. From the frequent occurrence of the names Flavia and Flavius in the inscriptions in the Catacombs, many members of the Flavian family must have become Christians. Many of these Christian graves are undoubtedly from the first century. It was not common to date the inscriptions on the graves, but we have at least three from the first century bearing dates. Christianity had a strong hold in Rome before the year 100. Everything that we know of Clemens and Domitilla goes to show that they were both Christians, for these charges which were made against them are the same that were made against the Christians. They had to refrain from any share in the affairs of state, and consequently they were charged with indifference to the state. Our duties as citizens sit lightly on us, but the Roman regarded his duties as a citizen as the highest and holiest imaginable. They were at the same time religious duties, because of the intimate relations existing between the state and her gods. No wonder, then, that the Christians gave so great offense by refusing to take part in public affairs.

But the most interesting fact is that Domitian, who was childless, had adopted the two sons of Clemens and Domitilla and designated them as his successors. Thus the presumptive heirs to the throne of the whole world were receiving a Christian training at the hand of Christian parents. But they were not destined to wear the crown. The hard fate of their parents seems to have overtaken them too, for after the death of their father and the banishment of their mother there is no further mention of them. It is of course idle to speculate as to what might have been the result if a Christian Emperor had come to the throne in the first century, instead of in the fourth. As it was, Christianity has hardly yet recovered from the evil effects of the so-called conversion of Constantine. A Christian Emperor in the first century might have done Christianity even a far greater injury.

CHAPTER IV.

THE CHURCH IN JERUSALEM DURING THE FIRST FOURTEEN YEARS.[1]

In some respects, the life of Jesus was a failure. It is said that he was sent as Messiah to the Jews, and it is certain that there was a widespread belief among them that their God had promised them a great deliverer. He was keenly sensible of the fact that he was a Jew. He loved Jewish history and was familiar with it. It was, to him, really a record of God's dealings with his people. He learned from it, apparently without difficulty, the lessons which history, when rightly understood, always teaches. He loved the land and especially the holy city. He was filled with a burning patriotism for his country, but he was of that small class of patriots who do not hesitate to rebuke the sins of their people and find the true greatness of a nation to consist in its moral and religious character. "O Jerusalem, Jerusalem, which killeth the prophets and stoneth them that are sent unto her! How often would I have gathered thy children together, even as a hen gathereth her own brood under her wings, and ye would not." It is a

---

[1] Read Acts i.–viii. 3 and xi.–xii. 25.

homely but touching figure, which reveals a heart full not only of love but also of despair. And during his "triumphal entry" into Jerusalem he wept aloud because this dear city was so blind to her highest and best interests. His tears show that he felt his inability to make the people understand the true character of the mutual relations that existed between God and his children. But the climax of his failure is expressed in the words, "He came unto his own and his own received him not." As a Messiah to the Jews his life was a failure, for as a nation they rejected him and his teachings. The current toward legalism was too strong for him. The religion which he taught, a religion of the heart, of the affections, of the will, and of the conscience, was for them too simple and at the same time too difficult. A religion which consists in the performance of certain acts and the obedience to certain commands is always more convenient and easier to practice, for it does not require the discipline and participation of the whole mental and spiritual nature of those who practice it.

But his life was not wholly a failure, for there were some who received him and showed themselves to be susceptible to his teachings. The thought that Christ made few disciples is sometimes pushed too far. The Evangelists often tell us of some that believed on him. Only, when we read that many believed on him, we must not interpret it to mean that they believed all that the church has since expressed in her creeds.

In Acts i. 15, it is said that there were about a hundred and twenty such gathered together, but it by no means is implied that all his followers were present. In 1 Corinthians xv. 6, Christ is said to have appeared to more than five hundred persons at once. So that at this time he must have had quite a respectable number of disciples who were attached to him personally and accepted his teachings.

Compared with the whole nation, these numbers, although very small, yet show that his labors had met with some success. The failure was not total. Their strength lay not in their numbers, but in the work assigned them. "Ye shall be witnesses unto me." And five hundred or six hundred witnesses all bearing the same testimony to one man certainly ought to make a very strong case for him. And that is what all these did: they bore testimony to the unique character of Jesus. Not even Judas has been excused from this service, for his cry, "I have betrayed innocent blood," has been heard throughout all these centuries.

Their testimony may be summed up in a few words: "Jesus is the promised Messiah." That was always their text: everything else was either proof of this or inference from it. This is the most prominent and frequently repeated statement in the writings of the New Testament. It is the constant theme of all the writers. They drew their proofs of it from many sources. If any passage of the Old Testament could be made to refer to him or to any event in his life, it was triumphantly quoted as a proof of his Messiahship. The method of interpretation then in vogue was the allegorical, and they were guided generally not by the original meaning of the author, but asked simply if the language could in any way be made to apply to the event in hand. In this way they applied many passages to him which we, without their guidance, would not regard as real proofs of his Messiahship. That, however, is only evidence of the deep impression which Christ had made on them. From their intercourse and companionship with him they knew that he was the Messiah, and hence, had no difficulty in finding proofs of it in the Old Testament.

They knew of his life, and that, too, furnished proofs of his Messiahship. His life and his teachings all showed that he had stood in a peculiar relation to God. The principal proof of this was to be found in the fact that, although he had been put to death, he was now alive again. Because of his obedience God had raised him from the dead, and had exalted him to the place of honor and dignity at his right hand. In fact they rested their whole case on this. The accounts which we have of the resurrection and of the intercourse of the risen Jesus with his disciples contain many difficulties. It is not easy to fit them together chronologically. According to some of them, Christ is very much like a disembodied spirit; he appears and disappears at will, he passes through closed doors, and shows that he is in every way free from all the physical limitations which had hemmed in his former existence. His body is no longer flesh and blood, but has crossed the boundary line which separates between the world of spirit and the world of sense. But, on the other hand, he is represented as having the same body with all its former characteristics and functions unchanged. He can be handled, he eats and drinks, and performs these acts for the purpose of convincing his doubting disciples of his identity. In this way he is represented as passing from the one state to the other, and we are left in doubt as to many things, because we are unable to see how a body could partake of these so contradictory characteristics at one and the same time. But one thing is secure, high above all doubt; the disciples *believed* that he was alive again. That fact cannot be questioned.

We must remember that the Twelve were children of their age. They shared in the political hopes and expectations of their people. Even to the last, they looked forward to the time when they would be the great ones in the Messiah's kingdom. Only a few days before the death of Christ, on the way up to Jerusalem to the last passover, they had quarreled by the way about the positions of honor which each hoped to obtain. When their teacher was arrested, like cowards they all fled for their lives. They did not wish even to confess that they had ever known him. Only one of them had the courage to witness his death. Fearful of the authorities, they met in secret and mourned and wept. Their leader was dead and his cause had died with him. Now they could only say that they *had hoped* that he would restore Israel to power. They no more expected to see Christ alive again than they expected the heavens to fall. The accounts of his first appearances were called " idle tales," and it was only with the greatest difficulty and the most convincing proofs that they all came to believe that he really was alive. It was a tremendous surprise to them, but they all came to believe it. It was for them the one great, irrefutable proof of the Messiahship of Jesus. God had borne testimony to the peculiar relationship existing between himself and Jesus by raising him from the dead and exalting him to his right hand. This formed the burden of all their utterances, and without it the success and power of Christianity would have been impossible.

They believed and declared this from the very first. Aside from the account which we have in the Acts, there are indirect evidences which show that this was the original belief of the disciples. Paul's conversion falls within five or six years, possibly within four years, of the date of the death of Jesus. And yet Paul had persecuted the Christians for their belief in the resurrection. It was an appearance of the risen Jesus that changed him from a bitter persecutor to an ardent apostle and firm believer in the crucified but risen Lord. Paul based everything on this fact, for " If Christ hath not been raised then is our preaching vain."

In 1 Corinthians xv. 3–8 ff., we have preserved the oldest written tradition in regard to the resurrection.[1] Here, in the most solemn and we might say official way, Paul declares that this was the common and universally accepted belief of the Christians. "For I delivered unto you first of all that which also I received, how that Christ died for our sins according to the Scriptures; and that he was buried; and that he hath been raised on the third day according to the Scriptures: and that he appeared to Cephas; then to the twelve; then he appeared to above five hundred brethren at once, of whom the greater part remain until now, but some are fallen asleep; then he appeared to James; then to all the apostles; and last of all, as unto one born out of due time, he appeared to me also." Paul appeals triumphantly to the five hundred to whom Christ had appeared at one time. Is it probable that five hundred persons would have one and the same vision?

To be sure, Paul does not appeal to the empty tomb, but to the many witnesses, a majority of whom were still alive, and what to us is of more value still, to his own sight of the risen Christ. He makes no difference between the appearance of Christ to the others and to himself. They had all seen him. They were all persuaded that he was alive and that God had established him in a position of glory and power. And it was this

[1] This letter was written between 55 and 57, while the Gospels and the Acts were not written for several years afterwards.

belief which filled them with enthusiasm, and was the mainspring of all their efforts to build up his kingdom.

The narrative of the choice of Matthias is interesting for several reasons. It shows that there were more than the twelve disciples that had followed Christ throughout his whole ministry. Here at least two such are mentioned, and we are not told whether there were others or not. This is the last time that the use of the lot is mentioned. This was common among the Jews. According to the religious conceptions in the Old Testament, it was regarded as a direct appeal to God, who is represented as ordering its practice and controlling it. But after the occurrence of Pentecost the lot is no longer used among the Christians, since it was the common belief that they all possessed, and were guided by, the Holy Spirit.

The account accords, too, with the general statement in the Gospels, in that Peter is represented as the spokesman and leader among the apostles. The election of one to take the place of Judas along with the Twelve throws a peculiar light on their mental condition. It shows that they attached great importance to the position which they held because of the rôle they were to play in the new state which was to include the twelve tribes. Undoubtedly, they still expected that they would be the great ones in this kingdom, and hence it was necessary that their number be complete. It shows that they thought of their mission as political, and as being directed first of all, if not exclusively, to the Jews. But the visions of greatness in which they indulged they never realized. The honor which they expected as leaders passed to others who showed by their actions that they better understood the spirit of Christ and his teachings. Others led the way in the work of preaching the gospel and carrying it to the ends of the earth.

From the title of the book, "The Acts of the Apostles," we should expect to find in it some account of the lives and labors of all the Twelve. It is a matter of much surprise, then, to find that nine of them are not so much as even named again after this first chapter. In the twelfth chapter the death of James is briefly recorded. John is barely mentioned three times. In all, not more than three or four chapters are taken up with a recital of Peter's labors. The disciples, much as we are accustomed to exalt them, created no place in history for themselves. To all intents and purposes they are but a list of names. We are at a loss to know how to explain this. Was it because they were still so Jewish that they were practically useless for the work of propagating the gospel? Were they men of so little importance and value personally that they at once dropped out of sight? Or did they labor earnestly, faithfully, and successfully and, like many another noble one, fail to find a biographer to record their deeds for the admiration of all posterity?

The temple in Jerusalem was built on a large area which contained many other buildings, halls, and arcades, which were used by the crowds of worshipers and visitors as lounging and resting-places. It was probably in one of these that the hundred and twenty disciples were gathered together on the day of Pentecost. The event described so rhetorically in the second chapter has always been regarded as epoch-making in the history of the Christian church. It has been much written about, and there are as many theories concerning it as there are authors that have written about it. Although it is full of difficulties from one point of view, if we follow the narrative three things seem to be clear. The first is that the Holy Spirit was given to all that were present. The extraordinary manifestations, whatever their character was, were not confined to the Twelve, but all alike were made partakers of them. The Spirit came upon all. "And there appeared unto them tongues parting asunder, like as of fire; and it sat upon *each* one of them. And they were *all* filled with the Holy Spirit." This is of tremendous importance, for it marks the beginning of a new era in religious development. According to the representations of the Old Testament, the Spirit of God had been given only to single favored individuals, not to all. Only the leaders, the kings, the prophets, and the priests could hope to have this great honor. The possession of the Holy Spirit, limited thus to a few in the Old Testament, was by the event of this day declared to be for all. The Spirit of God took up his abode in the individual believer, and each one is thereby made the dwelling-place of God himself.

What is this but a different form of statement of the truth which Christ taught, that God is our Father, and we as his children have direct access to Him without the intervention of others. A child-like, loving trust and reverence will cause us to walk in his spirit, and his spirit to dwell in us, and will make possible for each one the same deep, strengthening intercourse with God which Jesus himself enjoyed. The heathen thought of God as an enemy that must be propitiated: the Jew thought of God as the father of the nation; but Christ taught that He sustains the relation of father to each individual. This utterly destroyed priesthood. There is no need of priestly mediation between the believer and his God, for he is no longer to be kept as a minor or ward under religious guardians. There is no man, or class of men, that possesses the peculiar priestly privilege of mediating between God and his people. No one has a monopoly in supplying God's grace, for all his children have his spirit, and the way is open between Him and them. It is this that makes all believers kings and priests unto God.

The progress of Christianity was now made possible, for it was shown to be wholly independent of any man or class of men. Not even the Twelve could control it, for the Holy Spirit who was to govern all was possessed by all. This is really the basis for the principles of the freedom of conscience and the right of private judgment in matters of religion. No Christian may give his conscience or his judgment into the keeping of another, whether his priest or his pastor. They belong to himself; they are gifts from God, to whom he is responsible for their proper use. They are personal, and cannot be sublet to any one. When the church, in the course of time, took on a fixed form of government and adopted a creed, it usurped these rights of the individual. All had to yield unquestioning obedience to the priesthood, and no one dared say his conscience or his judgment was his own. If he did he was punished with excommunication, and might even consider himself fortunate if he escaped with his life. It is one of the great blessings resulting from the Reformation and the long struggles that it brought about, that the individual again got back his conscience and the right of private judgment which had been so long usurped.

It is evident, too, from the record that various languages were spoken. That is certainly what the author means to say. We are not to suppose, however, that he means that each one spoke all these languages, but that one spoke one, another another, so that one after another of them was heard. However surprising this may be, or whatever explanation of it may be accepted, it can hardly be doubted that this is the import of the language used.[1] This passage was for a long time supposed to declare that the early disciples had the supernatural gift of speaking any foreign language which was necessary for their mission work. But there is no trace of such a thing in the history of the period. On the contrary every indication that we have would show that they did not possess such powers. For tradition has inseparably associated Mark with Peter as his interpreter. And when Paul and Barnabas were in Lystra, and the people were preparing to offer them divine honors, they were not able to understand what was said in the language of the country, but it was necessary for it to be explained to them.

The third thing which seems to be clear from the text is that this "speaking with tongues" was accompanied by strange actions of the speakers. For those living in Jerusalem there would be nothing surprising in the fact that in a company of a hundred and twenty persons there should be several languages spoken. That a man should speak a foreign language would by no means be sufficient ground for saying that he was "full of new wine." Besides, Jerusalem was a very Babel of tongues;

[1] The most simple and common explanation offered by those who cannot accept this as real history is, that the author who wrote so many years after the event did not understand the expression which he found in his sources of information, but thought that to "speak with other tongues" meant to speak other languages, and so in describing the occurrence decked out his rhetorical narrative with these details as he supposed they must have taken place.

it was nothing remarkable to hear foreign languages spoken there all the time. We must look for another explanation of the surprise of the crowd that was gathered about them, and of the mocking taunt, "these men are full of new wine."

Our only source of knowledge about the speaking with tongues is in the fourteenth chapter of First Corinthians. If we put together some of the statements there made we shall be able to form some idea of what this peculiar phenomenon was. "For he that speaketh in a tongue speaketh not unto men, but unto God; for no man understandeth; but in the spirit he speaketh mysteries," ver. 2. "Now I would have you all speak with tongues, but rather that ye should prophesy: and greater is he that prophesieth than he that speaketh with tongues, except he interpret, that the church may receive edifying," ver. 5. "For if I pray in a tongue, my spirit prayeth, *but my understanding is unfruitful*," ver. 14. "If any man speaketh in a tongue, let it be by two, or at the most three, and that in turn; and let one interpret," ver. 27. It is clear from these passages that the speaker did not address the congregation, for his words were not understood by others. His mysterious, unintelligible utterances were spoken as a kind of prayer or address to God. At the time, he himself seems not to have known what he was saying, for his understanding was "unfruitful;" that is, he lost for the moment the use of his reason, he was not conscious of what he was saying, but was in such a physical and mental condition that he had no control over his tongue. Sometimes he himself could afterwards interpret to others what he had said while in this strange state. At other times some one of those present could interpret, but it often happened that there was no one present who could explain what he had said. Such a strange condition reminds one of the story of Balaam's prophecies recorded in Numbers. When he prophesied he lost all control of his will, his tongue uttered what it would, his understanding was inactive, he fell down, his eyes were open but he saw nothing, and he was wholly unconscious of what he said and did. He was in what is called an ecstatic condition.

If we read the account now with all this in mind, the astonishment of the crowd and the charge of drunkenness are easily explained. As one after another of the hundred and twenty was seized by the Spirit and filled with rapturous enthusiasm, they each passed into a condition resembling this ecstatic state and gave utterance to their praises, while their actions were strange, resembling those of drunken men. It was their strange gestures, then, that caused some to mock and say that they were full of new wine.

This strange occurrence at any rate filled the disciples with courage and boldness. There was no longer any fear among them, but they are represented as speaking plainly and boldly from this time on. It also impressed many of the hearers, and much of the success of the day is to be attributed not wholly to the address of Peter, but in part at least to this. It is agreed, too, by all, that this event had also a symbolic use. The use of all languages indicated that the message was for all tongues and all peoples. All languages were hereby sanctified for the purpose of spreading the gospel. It was a token in advance that the gospel would be preached in all tongues. It symbolized its universality.

The language used in regard to the possessions of the members of the new society deserves careful examination. There are several very strong general statements in the text. "And all that believed were together, and had all things common; and they sold their possessions and goods, and parted them to all, according as any man had need" (Acts ii. 44, 45). "And the multitude of them that believed were of one heart and soul: and not one of them said that aught of the things which he possessed was his own; but they had all things common. For neither was there among them any that lacked: for as many as were possessors of lands or houses sold them, and brought the prices of the things that were sold, and laid them at the apostles' feet: and distribution was made unto each, according as any one had need" (Acts iv. 32, 34, 35). It would be difficult to make stronger or more sweeping statements than are contained in these quotations, and it looks as if they were wholly justified, who have spoken of this as the "Jerusalem communism." For if the words are to be taken at their face value without careful study of their surroundings, we have here complete communism. All personal rights seem to be gone. But the narrative furnishes some very important limitations to this view. It was not *required* of the members that they surrender their property for the benefit of their brethren. For Peter said to Ananias, " While it remained, did it not remain thine own? And after it was sold was it not in thy power?" Such a gift was wholly voluntary. Ananias might have been a member " in good standing " without surrendering any of his possessions. It was not regarded as a term of fellowship, and it was not a condition of membership in the new church. There is not much danger in a communism that is voluntary, for it is not likely to become extremely popular. It was also partial, for a little later we find that Mary, the mother of Mark, had a house in Jerusalem (Acts xii. 12). Even of Ananias and Sapphira it is said that they sold *a* possession. It by no means follows that that was all they had. This communism was also local. It was confined wholly to Jerusalem. There is not a single trace of it outside that city.[1] On the contrary, every bit of information which we possess goes to show that there was no such practice anywhere else. In 1 Cor. xvi. 2, Paul asks that each of the Corin-

---

[1] Perhaps in 1 Thess. iv. 11, and 2 Thess. iii. 10, 11, there is a germ or beginning of such a movement, but it is most severely rebuked by Paul.

thian congregation should lay aside as he has prospered. There is evidently no communism there. Besides, whatever else this communism in Jerusalem was, it was a failure, for Paul and others were continually making collections for the " poor saints," up at Jerusalem. It is not impossible that the Jewish Christians in Palestine received the nickname of the " poor " (for that is what Ebionite means), which clung to the remnant of them that continued to observe the Jewish law and peculiarities during the first centuries. It need hardly be said that any ism that leads to beggary and the poor-house is self-condemned, since it defeats the end for which it is supposed to exist.

We have, however, in this account a fine proof of the strength of the new ideas that were preached. It shows what a new and deep feeling of brotherhood, equality, and unity was produced among the believers by the message of the risen Christ, who would presently come in person to establish his kingdom and receive his followers. It is probable, too, that the belief and hope that he would soon return influenced them, and they parted with their possessions all the more willingly because they thought it was only for a short time. This was not at all uncommon in the early church. There were many who were so overpowered by the teaching that they willingly sold all that they had and went out into the world devoting themselves to the work of spreading the gospel.

We can also see that it must have been a very

popular thing to do in Jerusalem. A man who gave so liberally would certainly be lionized. We are all disposed to show a good deal of veneration to those who benefit us largely by their gifts. The liberal man must be a very bad man indeed, if he is not popular, for such charity always covers a multitude of sins. But Eastern peoples are especially obsequious to their benefactors, and undoubtedly all who gave so liberally of their possessions would be at once exalted to a high position of influence and honor. It was this that offered temptation to those that were ambitious, and introduced the first cool deception and calculating fraud into the happy and contented congregation. Ananias and Sapphira coveted the popularity and high position which they saw those enjoying who had thus given all they possessed to their brethren and were spending their lives in the services of the gospel. But this popularity came high; it would cost them their possessions. And such a price they were unwilling to pay. So they tried to get it by means of hypocrisy. They professed to give all that they had received for the piece of property which they had sold. Hypocrites are a hindrance in any good movement. The better the movement, the greater the danger from such people, and the more injurious are their presence and influence. A few individuals of such character, who in this way had got leading positions in the young church, could have ruined it. The danger was great, the remedy severe.

Attention has already been called to the fact that there were many Jews outside of Palestine who had taken much of the Greek culture, and were consequently called Hellenists. They were, however, despised by the Jews in Palestine, because they lived outside the Holy Land. For according to their conception, all foreign lands were unclean and all those who lived in them were necessarily contaminated and were as far as possible to be shunned. But the Jews in the Diaspora never forgot Jerusalem; and it was their last wish to return thither that they might there die and be buried under the shadow of its walls. It was only natural that those who returned to Jerusalem from the same province or part of the world would to a certain extent, at least, form a separate society. And so we find that those from a particular province generally had their own synagogue, where they could meet and continue their friendships which had been begun in a foreign land.

It was this religious pride of the Palestinian members of the church that first disturbed its peace. The widows of the Hellenists, that is, of these Greek Jews, were slighted in the distribution of the alms. Those that had charge of the funds were not impartial in their treatment of the poor members who needed help. The other poor were cared for, but the poor widows who had been so unfortunate as to have lived in an unclean land were despised and neglected. We do not know who had been attending to this work, but their conduct was an offense against the principles of brotherhood and equality which had been at first received with such joy and enthusiasm. The line between Hellenists and Palestinian Jews had seemed to be effaced, but this injustice and partiality at once awakened the old feelings, the party lines were quickly drawn again, and the Hellenists stood on one side and the Palestinian Jews on the other. As they could not settle the difficulty, they appealed to the apostles. These refused to give up the service of the word for the service of the tables, but proposed that seven men of tried character be chosen who should have charge of this work. It is probable, from the names, that a majority of these were Hellenists. Of the seven only two, Stephen and Philip, are afterwards mentioned. Absolutely nothing further is known of the others.

The national and religious narrowness of the Jews in Palestine has already been spoken of. In their eyes three things were especially holy; the land, the law, and the temple. Palestine was holy, while every other land was unclean. No one could live outside of Palestine and serve God. They believed that God loved Palestine, but every other country was an abomination in his sight. As to the law, they had made an idol of it. It was holy in and of itself. It was the last and highest expression of God's holy will. He was the most holy and the most acceptable to God who most nearly kept its every command. Since the worship of God by sacrifice had been forbidden in every other part of Palestine, the temple had increased in importance, and it is scarcely necessary to speak of the idolatrous veneration with which the Jew regarded it. These three things had an innate holiness, they were to endure forever. For when the Messiah should come, Palestine was to enjoy his favor and presence, while the rest of the world was to be subjected and ruled with a rod of iron. The law, now so limited, he was to make binding on the whole earth, while the temple was to become the temple for the whole world, the one place where men might offer sacrifices and pay their vows to God. They identified the interests of religion with those of Judaism; in fact, Judaism and religion were synonymous. They thought that religion could not exist in any other form than in that of Judaism. There is an immense gulf between this conception of religion and that of Christ, according to whom religion consists in the attitude of the heart toward God.

It is a fact worth noting, because characteristic of the period, that not one of the Twelve, but a Hellenist, was the first to discover that Christ's teachings made an end of Judaism. All had supposed that Christianity was but the completion of Judaism, not its supplanter. Stephen was the first to understand the true character of Christianity, and he at once saw that the Jewish forms could not exist as a part of Christianity. He perceived that Christ had shown that religion was a matter of the heart; that he had freed religion from every external, and thereby had made of it a universal religion. For he had freed it from every national and local limitation, had shown that the true religion is possible everywhere, and is to be found wherever a heart, filled with penitence and humility, and trusting in God as a loving Father, daily strives to serve Him by fulfilling the duties which He gives it to do. He declared that the law of Moses was no longer binding, and that the temple was not necessary for the worship of God.

Stephen's speech is aimed against the Jews and the false value which was attached to the land, the law, and the temple. He proves to them from their own history that God's grace is not bound to these. They cannot be essential to God's favor, for He has shown his grace to some outside of the Holy Land, before the law was given, and before the temple was built. God had chosen Abraham long before he had come into Palestine, and had cared for his children while they were in the strange land of Egypt. And so Stephen reviews their history, and shows that God had gradually revealed his will, that there had been successive stages in the revelation of himself. Progress had been the principle of his dealings with them. At first He had given them only the sign of circumcision, then after a long time the law had been added. Then the Tabernacle had been built, but after hundreds of years it had given place to the temple. And now there is a new and higher stage introduced by Jesus, his Messiah. As the temple had replaced the Tabernacle, so Judaism was replaced by Christianity. Each had done its work in its time, and served the purpose for which it had been instituted. But there was nothing in them which made it necessary that they should be binding forever. They were not holy of themselves, for holiness is only of the heart, it cannot attach to things. Why was it, then, that the Jews had rejected the Messiah, and now refused to follow in his teachings? For Stephen the answer was very easy. They had never willingly accepted the new. They had always held to the old and refused to listen to the new truths which He had sent them by his messengers. Always rebellious, they had never recognized God's hand in the changes and new institutions, but, spiritually blind, they held with fanatical zeal to the old. They had always resisted, and in the treatment of his Messiah had given but another proof of the hardness of their hearts. Stephen made the charge very pointed, but they did not permit him to finish it. Enraged at these charges and at his blasphemous words against the temple and the law, they rushed upon him, hustled him out of the city, and stoned him. He suffered death at the hands of such a maddened and fanatical mob as had once demanded of Pilate the death of Jesus. But in this case there was no trial; the mob passed and executed its own sentence without appeal to the Roman authorities.

Stephen was the first to distinguish between Christianity and Judaism, and his sharp criticism of the law and the temple aroused such hostility as to bring about not only his own death but also severe persecution of the Christians. The Jews were suddenly made aware of the fact that this was an heretical sect that was growing up among them. The persecution, however, had at least two good results. It greatly hastened, as we have already seen, the spread of Christianity, by scattering the Christians abroad and thrusting them forth into the work of propagating their belief, and it helped to develop the self-consciousness of Christianity. They were persecuted for their belief in the Christ, which was the very thing that distinguished them from other Jews. It emphasized the difference between them, and marked the beginning of a new period in the development of Christianity from a Jewish sect into a world religion. From this time on, Christianity became more and more differentiated from Judaism, threw off its Jewish wrappings, and appeared as a complete and independent religion.

Herod Agrippa I., the grandson of Herod the Great, had with some difficulty succeeded, in the year 41 A. D., in getting the title of King, and all Palestine for his kingdom. In Rome he had lived as the Romans. But it was necessary for him to win the good will of the Jews; so there was a decided change in his conduct when he came among them as their king. He pretended to be a Pharisee of the Pharisees, living outwardly at least according to the law, and in every way seeking to please the Jews. It is entirely in accordance with his policy that he should cause the Christians trouble, especially if the Jews should make charges against them. It is impossible to believe that it was really a matter of faith with him, so his contemptibility appears in a strong light, because of the fact that for the sake of popularity he persecuted at the desire of the Jews. His most prominent victim was James the brother of John, who suffered martyrdom about the year 44. Peter also was seized, but in a remarkable way escaped the threatened death.

Josephus (Antiquities xix. 8) gives an account of the death of this Herod, with which our narrative in the Acts in general agrees. According to Josephus he was suddenly seized with severe pains, and died after five days of great agony.

Scattered throughout these twelve chapters are several general statements in regard to the peaceful and prosperous condition of the Christian community in Jerusalem.[1] These are not to be pressed too far, for there was, as we have seen, some opposition and persecution. The hostility of the Jewish hierarchy is represented as increasing, though kept in bounds for awhile by the favor which the Christians enjoyed with the common people. This favor is attributed to two things: first, the beneficent miracles of the apostles; and second, the

[1] See Acts ii. 42–47, and v. 12–16 and 42.

conservatism of the new movement. They by no means neglected the Jewish institutions, but at the regular hours of prayer were found in the temple, and undoubtedly observed the feasts and fasts, and outwardly in no way distinguished themselves from the Jews about them.

CHAPTER V.

BREAKING THE JEWISH BONDS.[1]

THE attitude of the majority of the Jewish Christians and of the Mother Church at Jerusalem toward the heathen has been made sufficiently plain. Undoubtedly there were many who disregarded their opinions and preached the gospel to the heathen, and associated with them without any regard to the requirements of the law. But of all these Paul is the only one of whom we have any detailed information, and more than that, he is the only one who attempted to tell *why* the law is no longer binding on those who believe in Christ. The history of the Apostolic Church is practically the history of Paul, because we have no certain information about the labors of others. It will be best to gather up here all the scattered personal notices of him, that we may get as clear a picture of him as possible.

Paul always spoke of his birthplace with patriotic pride, and justly too, for Tarsus was indeed "no mean city." It was an important centre of trade, and consequently rich. It was a place of

[1] Read Acts ix. 1-30 and xiii.-xiv.

great culture, for it was the seat of the third university of the world. There were many learned professors there, whose students were much sought after as tutors and professors in other places. In studying the character and life of Paul it is of the utmost importance to remember that he grew up in the atmosphere of a great and busy city, for it greatly influenced him in many ways. His cosmopolitan culture he owed to the influence of his training and surroundings in Tarsus. It was always easy for him to associate with all classes, with the cultured and refined as well as with the common people. He could deal with men, with individuals, and with the masses. In his letters, his politeness and thoughtfulness for others are everywhere apparent. He knew how to turn a compliment and say pleasant things to those whom he wished to win. It is impossible not to see a great difference between him and the Twelve in this respect, and this is due largely to the fact that he was a child of the city, while they were of the country.

He is known to us by two names, Saul and Paul. A good deal of ingenuity has been expended in trying to explain why he is called Saul up to a certain place in the Acts (xiii. 9), and after that, with rare exceptions, Paul. Most writers have supposed that he actually changed his name; but that is extremely improbable, and the difficulty is easily explained in another way. It was common for the Jews, especially those who lived in the

Diaspora, to have two names, the one Jewish, the other Greek; and often these two were much alike in sound. One who bore the name of Joshua would also be called Jason. Undoubtedly Paul bore both names from his childhood. It is not to be supposed that the author of the Acts wrote this book simply from his own knowledge of the events or from hearsay. He himself tells us in the prologue to his Gospel that he had used written sources in its composition, and as in the Acts he narrates events that were far apart in both time and place, it is very probable that he would look about for written sources for this work also. The first chapters of the Acts differ from the later ones, and there are several peculiarities which make it probable that he got much of his information from an Aramaic writing which was a narrative of some of the events in Palestine, and in this the name Saul was used. But later, as he labored more and more among the heathen, he made use exclusively of the name Paul. The same thing is apparent in the case of John Mark. At first both his names are given, but later he is simply called Mark, because, as he was among the heathen, his Jewish name dropped out of use. A similar example is found in Col. iv. 11, where Jesus is said also to have had the name of Justus.

The time of his birth and consequently his age are unknown. There are only two passages that give any hint as to how old he was. At the time of the violent death of Stephen, probably 33 or 34, he is spoken of as a "young man," a term which was generally applied to those between eighteen and thirty years of age. But in common speech it was by no means used with such exactness that we can conclude that Paul was no more than thirty nor less than eighteen. In his letter to Philemon (ver. 9) written about 62 A. D., he speaks of himself as " Paul the aged." It is scarcely probable that he would use such language of himself unless he was at least fifty years old; but the expression is indefinite, and apparently Paul applied it to himself in a half-playful way.

Although a Jew he was a Roman citizen :[1] that is, he had all the rights which an inhabitant of Rome possessed. We do not know how his father obtained this right, whether by service or by purchase. Of his family we know almost nothing. He had a sister who lived at Jerusalem; or, at least, her son was there. His parents were of the tribe of Benjamin, and although living among the heathen, seem to have remained Jews of the strictest sort. More than once Paul speaks of his early life and training, and always emphasizes the fact that he had been brought up in accordance with the strictest rules of Phariseeism. He was one of those Pharisees who with his whole heart endeavored to keep the law.

Although he lived in a university city, his education was wholly Jewish. The Phariseeism of his

---

[1] Acts xvi. 37, xxii. 28, and elsewhere.

family would prevent his mingling with the students and professors of a heathen school. Moreover, he does not in his writings show any trace of the Greek education of the period. To be sure, he quotes the Greek poets. "For we are also his offspring" (Acts xvii. 28) is a line from Aratus, a Cilician, and therefore a countryman of Paul. And Cleanthus of Mysia had also given expression to the same thought. "Evil company doth corrupt good manners" (1 Cor. xv. 33) is a quotation from Menander. And the very uncomplimentary saying about the Cretans is from Epimenides: "Cretans are always liars, evil beasts, idle gluttons" (Titus 1-12). But three quotations from Greek poets by no means prove that he had a Greek education. In the first place, they are all of a proverbial character, and likely to be in every one's mouth, just as Shakespeare is quoted every day by many who have never read one of his plays. Besides, it must be remembered that Paul had been for years associating in the most intimate way with Greeks, and it would be strange indeed if he had not become master of many such quotations which were so commonly used. This was by no means a Greek education, for that consisted in the study of philosophy, literature, and rhetoric. His style is Aramaic rather than Greek. It is far from elegant, and lacks clearness. He piles up words after the Aramaic fashion in such a way that it is almost impossible to tell what their connection and relation are. From his style, one would almost be persuaded to believe that he always thought in Aramaic, and had to translate it into Greek.

It was determined that he should become a Rabbi, and for the purpose of completing his education he went to Jerusalem, where he chose for his instructor Gamaliel, who was famous as one of the most liberal and learned Rabbis of his times. But whatever else he may have got from his teacher, he did not get his moderate discriminating spirit. As a Hellenist Rabbi, he studied the Old Testament in both Hebrew and Greek. His quotations from the Old Testament correspond more closely to the Greek text of the Septuagint than to the Hebrew text. The Aramaic translations of the Old Testament existed orally, though probably they had not yet been reduced to writing. He got something from these, for in Gal. iii. 19, he speaks of the law as having been "ordained through angels," a fact which is not stated in the Hebrew text of the Old Testament, but is an addition which is found in the Targums. Again in Gal. iv. 29, he says that Esau persecuted Jacob, which is also an addition that is found in the Targums, but not in the Hebrew. He heard also from his teacher the traditional exegesis, which consisted mainly in repeating what former noted Rabbis had said. Each teacher quoted the opinions of others and then added his own. As a debater he has seldom been equaled. His skill in reasoning is astonishing; he heaps up arguments in the most prodigal way, as if he knew that his supply was unlimited.

Everything, however unpromising, was put under tribute, and had to furnish him with proofs and arguments. He turned his opponents' weapons and made them do service for himself.

It was customary for every Rabbi to learn a trade, for according to the law they were not allowed to receive pay for their advice and instruction. But there were many ways of evading this, and probably very few Rabbis actually lived from the income of their trade. Paul had already learned the trade which was so common in his own home, that of weaving coarse cloth of the long wool of the Cilician goats and cutting it into the necessary patterns for tents. How long he was in Jerusalem it is impossible to tell. We do not know whether he left Jerusalem after completing his studies and went as a young Rabbi to Tarsus, or to some other city. He may have remained in Jerusalem, perhaps, as Rabbi in the synagogue "of them of Cilicia and Asia" (Acts vi. 9). Nor do we know whether he had heard John the Baptist or Jesus. There is only one passage in all his writings which can be interpreted to mean that he had seen Jesus; "even though we have known Christ after the flesh, yet now we know him so no more" (2 Cor. v. 16). This seems to say that Paul had seen Christ in the flesh, that is, before his death, and all the interpretations of the words which exclude this meaning are somewhat forced and unsatisfactory. Apparently he had seen Jesus while he was going about as a traveling Rabbi, and had thought of him accordingly. But now, since he had seen him as the risen and glorified Messiah, he could think of him only as such.

In Acts xxvi. 10, Paul says that when the Christians were put to death he gave his " vote " against them, and from this it has been supposed by many that he was a member of the Sanhedrin. But in parallel passages, when speaking of the same thing, a more general expression is used. It is said that he " consented " to their death. It is probable, therefore, that " vote " is to be taken not in its technical, but in its general sense, and that it means simply that Paul heartily sympathized with the harsh measures used to destroy heresy. Besides, according to the law, no man who was without wife and children could be elected to the Sanhedrin. But we do not know whether this was a dead letter or not. Paul seems not to have been married. There is no mention of wife or children. On the contrary, in 1 Cor. vii. 8, he advises the unmarried and widows to remain as he is, that is, unmarried.

As to his appearance, we are left to indirect statements and inferences. An authentic portrait of Paul would be one of the most interesting things imaginable, but no such portrait exists. He was probably small of stature, for his opponents in Corinth said that he could write blustering, threatening letters, as if he were able to do great things, but his bodily presence was weak and insignificant. At Lystra, where the enthusiastic inhabitants were going to pay divine honors to him and Barnabas, he was called Hermes, while Barnabas was called Zeus. In all works of art, Zeus is represented as of large stature and with a heavy beard, while Hermes is small and beardless. In the Acts of Paul and Thecla, the first Christian romance, written about 150 A. D., there is a description of Paul which is probably based on a true tradition. In this he is described as "a man small in size, bald-headed, bandy-legged, well-built, with eyebrows meeting, rather long-nosed, and with motions full of grace."

In Galatians, and especially in his letters to the Corinthians, there is much said about his sufferings and infirmities. A sigh as of bodily pain and sickness seems to be heard through them all. His body was marked by rods and scourges and racked by persecutions, and his health was broken by the many hardships which he had experienced. He must have had a strong body and great vigor of constitution to endure all the violence that had been done him.

Besides this, he had also a special suffering, some bodily ailment, which he called "a thorn in the flesh, a messenger of Satan to buffet me, that I should not be exalted overmuch" (2 Cor. xii. 7). What it was he does not clearly say, but it is not improbable that it was a severe affliction of the eyes. It must be remembered that at the time of his conversion he is said to have been blinded for some time. In his letter to the Galatians (iv. 13 ff.), he reminds them that it had not been his intention to preach the gospel to them, but because of sickness he was prevented from pursuing his journey, and had used the time of delay to make them acquainted with the way of life. His sickness was of such a character as to make it probable that the Galatians would despise him, and because of disgust for his bodily condition reject his message. But they had not been affected by this, for Paul bears them witness that they received him with honor, and were so devoted to him that if it had been possible, they would even have *plucked out their eyes* and given them to him. This expression, taken in connection with the fact that it was some bodily sickness which made it impossible for him to travel, but did not prevent him from carrying on his evangelistic work, makes it not improbable that it was some affection of the eyes. Again, in Acts xxiii. 5, Paul did not recognize the high priest, although he must have been very near him. The only explanation seems to be that he could not see clearly. Besides this, Paul did not write his own letters, but dictated them to some one else, and only at the end with his own hand added a few words, generally of salutation. At the end of several of his letters, he calls special attention to the fact that he was himself adding the last words. "The salutation of me, Paul, with my own hand, which is the token in every epistle, so I write" (2 Thess. iii. 17). He tells them that he always signed his letters and that his signature was the sign of genuineness. And in Galatians vi. 11, he says, "See with what *large* letters I am writing to you with my own hand." These words refer to what follows, and call attention to the peculiarity of his handwriting. Like one whose sight is dim, he could write only in large, scrawling letters. It seems to be clear, then, that he suffered from some affection of his eyes. This may have been the thorn of which he speaks, and especially, if this began about the time of his conversion, it would be a forcible reminder to him of his former opposition to Christ and his people. But whatever this thorn was, he regarded it as a painful, burdensome, and humiliating limitation in his work.[1]

His temperament is difficult to describe, because so varied, so full of opposite extremes. The saying, "The style is the man," may be applied to him as perhaps to no other. If you would form a good idea of him, read all his letters with this one thing in view. Note the rapid changes in him. How he opens his heart to the Philippians! Though in prison, his heart is full of sunshine, and his expressions of gratitude to them for their gift are simple, hearty, and touching. But here we have only one side of him. In Galatians and 2 Corinthians we have the whole man. It is in

[1] Krenkel is decidedly of the opinion that Paul was subject to epilepsy, and that this was the thorn of which he speaks. He has collected much material on the subject, but has not made a strong case at all.

these especially that the extremes in his nature are revealed lying side by side. It is in these that he displays such tenderness and gentleness, such joy and peace, such confidence and happiness, and at the same time such indignation and anger, such sorrow and unrest, such discontent and discouragement. In the same breath he writes the most biting sarcasm and the truest pathos. Words of irony and gratitude follow each other in quick succession from his pen. In one moment he is all anger and threats, the next he is all tenderness and beseeching. He could say hard and bitter as well as pleasant things. His feelings were most changeable, his faith most abiding. His ideas outran his utterance, and he often left one sentence unfinished and passed to another, hurried on by the flood of thoughts and rush of feelings. Naturally he was not of a harmonious nature. Men of such extremes never are. But he had obtained from God, in the school of Christ, that deeper harmony which made him what he was. The greatness of the work of grace in him is clearly shown in Phil. i. 12–26. He had personal enemies in Rome, some who were envious of him, and through envy and strife were preaching only that they might surpass him, and have a larger following and greater reputation among the Christians in Rome than he, but their envy did not move him. His only answer was " What then? Only that in every way, whether in pretense or in truth, Christ is proclaimed; and therein I rejoice, yea, and will rejoice." One feels his great heart throb in every line of his second letter to the Corinthians. He wrote it unwillingly, but the situation forced it from him. It is impossible not to feel his pain and anguish, as one reads this painful defense of himself. But his heart shines out through it all, and some of the passages in it are unsurpassable in their eloquent pathos. Who else could have written such words as these? "Are they Hebrews? so am I. Are they Israelites? so am I. Are they the seed of Abraham? so am I. Are they ministers of Christ? (I speak as one beside himself) I more; in labors more abundantly, in prisons more abundantly, in stripes above measure, in deaths oft. Of the Jews five times received I forty stripes save one. Thrice was I beaten with rods, once was I stoned, thrice I suffered shipwreck, a night and a day have I been in the deep; in journeyings often, in perils of rivers, in perils of robbers, in perils from my countrymen, in perils from the Gentiles, in perils in the city, in perils in the wilderness, in perils in the sea, in perils among false brethren; in labor and travail, in watchings often, in hunger and thirst, in fastings often, in cold and nakedness. Beside those things that are without, there is that which presseth upon me daily, anxiety for all the churches. Who is weak, and I am not weak? who is made to stumble, and I burn not?" (2 Cor. xi. 22-29). "Giving no occasion of stumbling in anything, that our ministration be not blamed; but in everything commending ourselves, as ministers of God, in much patience, in afflictions, in necessities, in distresses, in stripes, in imprisonments, in tumults, in labors, in watchings, in fastings; in pureness, in knowledge, in long-suffering, in kindness, in the Holy Ghost, in love unfeigned, in the word of truth, in the power of God; by the armor of righteousness on the right hand and on the left, by glory and dishonor, by evil report and good report; as deceivers, and yet true; as unknown, and yet well known; as dying, and behold we live; as chastened, and not killed; as sorrowful, yet alway rejoicing; as poor, yet making many rich: as having nothing, and yet possessing all things" (2 Cor. vi. 3–10).

The first mention made of him is in connection with the death of Stephen, Acts vii. 58. It is said, vi. 9, that Stephen disputed with men from two synagogues. The one of these was frequented by Libertines, Cyrenians, and Alexandrians. The Libertines were Jews who had been carried off to Rome as prisoners, but had been set free. The other synagogue was frequented by Cilicians and people from other parts of Asia Minor. Now Tarsus was in Cilicia, and it was quite natural that Paul should be connected with that synagogue. It is very probable, then, that Paul was one of the opponents of Stephen, and if he were the principal opponent it would account for the fact that the witnesses "laid down their clothes at the feet of a young man named Saul."

It is characteristic of him and of his zeal that

he himself went to the high priest and asked for a commission to persecute. It is probable that his connection with the death of Stephen was well known, and was looked upon as a recommendation of his fitness for the work. At any rate, something made them think that he would make a good heresy-hunter; so they granted his request, and gave him letters of recommendation, and authority to persecute, even far beyond the boundaries of Palestine. In many places the Jews had extraordinary jurisdiction, and special judicial rights, having courts of their own and following their own laws and methods of procedure; so that there is nothing surprising about this commission of Paul.

As a persecutor he showed great activity and ability. We have almost no details of his work, but some general statements give us a good idea of it. He imprisoned men and women, scourged some, and urged that others be put to death. In his persecuting zeal, he went to other cities and won great fame. The Christians at Damascus knew of his destructive work, and feared to trust him, although he claimed to have been converted. It was his glory then, because he thought he was pleasing God; but afterwards it was the source of unbounded sorrow to him. He seems never to have forgot it even for a moment. How often he quotes it against himself! He was not fit to be called an apostle, because he had persecuted the church of God. It kept him always humble, and was a constant spur to greater endeavors in his missionary work, that if possible he might make good all the damage he had done in his mad zeal.

Of his conversion we have three accounts in the Acts, besides some scattered references to it in his letters. "Have I not seen Jesus our Lord?" he asks the Corinthians (1 Cor. ix. 1). This is undoubtedly to be referred to the vision which he had of the risen Messiah at the time of his conversion. Again in the fifteenth chapter, when recounting the appearance of Jesus, he says, "And last of all, as unto one born out of due time, he appeared to me also." It is difficult to understand these words in any other way than that Paul believed that he had seen the Christ with his bodily eyes. But in Gal. i. 17 he uses language that is somewhat different: "But when it was the good pleasure of God to reveal his Son *in me*." This alone might be interpreted as a purely mental process. The three accounts in the Acts agree rather with the former than with the latter. They are found in chapters ix., xxii., and xxvi. There are some verbal differences, and the details are treated differently. But it is the same picture, although the colors vary. The differences are rhetorical, and do not affect the important part of the narrative.

In the ninth chapter it is said that the men *stood* speechless; according to the twenty-sixth, they all *fell* to the earth. In the ninth chapter they *heard the voice*, but *saw* no one; while in the twenty-second they *saw the light,* but *did not hear the voice.* In the ninth and twenty-second, *Paul is told to go into Damascus, and there it should be told him what he was to do.* But, according to the twenty-sixth, *Christ tells him at once what his mission is.* It is difficult to harmonize all these without doing violence to some of the language, but there are certain things that remain fixed in spite of these differences.

Leaving out of account the various things which are doubtful, those that are fixed may be summed up as follows: The time of the occurrence, about midday; the place, near Damascus; the purpose of the journey, to persecute the Christians; the sudden and unexpected appearance of Jesus before him, surrounded by a light which blinded Paul and symbolized the glory of his present exalted position as the Messiah at the right hand of God; the complete and instantaneous change in Paul's attitude to Jesus, — in one moment he was a persecutor, in the next he was a believer in his Messiahship; and lastly, his call to preach the gospel to the heathen. All these except the first two are corroborated more or less directly by those of Paul's letters, which are unquestionably authentic. However they may be explained, they can hardly be questioned as historical facts. Paul believed in the absolute reality of this appearance. It was not a vision or dream; he actually saw the glorified Christ. He had seen him just as the others had seen him. It certainly is a strong corroboration of this, that all Paul's thought centres about Jesus as the risen and glorified Messiah. It is not the man Jesus, who appeared as a humble and obedient servant, but the living, exalted Messiah that Paul preached. It was the fact that although Jesus had been put to death he still lived in heaven, that so changed Paul and convinced him of his Messiahship. And it is from this point of view that he formed all his opinions about him. All his theology is developed from this belief. There is absolutely no indication of any preparation for this sudden change in him; there is no period of doubt, hesitation, and inquiry preceding the change of his belief. He himself connected his conversion with the appearance of Jesus. From the same time and event he dates his call to the apostleship. From the very beginning he was the apostle to the Gentiles. He knew from that time what his work was to be. He was so sure of this that he never thought of saying anything about it to the Twelve, or to any one else. From Christ himself he received his command to go to the heathen; he did not need to have this sanctioned by any one of the Twelve. He did not think it necessary to know what the life of Christ had been, he did not ask about the details of it. They were to him unimportant. He knew that he had lived and died, but the important thing was that he was now alive. "His gospel" was all contained in that, for it is simply the interpretation and explanation of the death and resurrection of

Christ; and his death as well as everything else he interpreted in the light of the resurrection. Paul strove to explain and define these as no other writer of the New Testament, and it is on this account that theology is so largely based on Paul's writings.

In regard to Paul's conversion and the source of his gospel, it must be remembered that Paul was a Pharisee of the strictest type, and therefore had the same ideas, hopes, and expectations about the Messiah, his coming, his reign, and his attitude to the heathen, as prevailed among the Pharisees at that time. They believed that the coming of the Messiah was dependent on the condition of his people. Before he could appear, his people must be holy, must be justified by keeping the law perfectly, for that was the only way for the people to be justified. Justification consisted in the complete observance of the law. Holiness was the result of doing something, while Christ had said that it is of the heart and not of actions. It was this explanation of holiness that made the Pharisee so zealous for the law. This, then, was one radical point of difference, and hence the cause of enmity and opposition, between them and Jesus. This was one great stumbling-block in the way of the Jews. But a greater one was the death of Jesus on the cross. This was to Paul inexplicable. It was so contrary to their expectations, so different from their ideas of the unbroken reign of splendor which the royal Messiah should enjoy. It was treason to the Messiah to entertain such a thought of him.

Now Paul was so thoroughly persuaded of all this that he was persecuting all those who believed in the Messiahship of Jesus, when, on his way to Damascus, he was suddenly confronted by the one who he knew had died a violent and shameful death. But his appearance to him was proof that he was alive again. For Paul, there was no question about this fact, for he had seen him and talked with him. The fact that he was alive again put his death in a new light. It showed that it could not have been a misfortune, an unforeseen accident, but that it was a part of God's plan. His death must have been of his own free will, for otherwise who could injure God's Messiah? There were some passages in the Old Testament that had come to be applied to the Messiah which spoke of his sufferings. They had been obscured and disregarded because of the ideas which were prevalent in regard to his glory and power. But now their meaning was clear to Paul. The mysterious words of the prophet Isaiah, that the suffering Servant should make himself, his life (not *soul*, as it is commonly translated, but *self, life*), an offering for sin, were now explained by the death of Jesus, and the death of Jesus was explained by them. He was himself by his obedient death the sin-offering for his people, and thereby had obtained justification for them. It was a new idea that the Messiah should by his death justify his people.

Justification, then, was not to be got by the works of the law, but by the work and death of the Messiah. It was wholly his work, the people had but to receive it. It follows necessarily, then, that he could bestow it on whom he would. No one could have any *claim* to what was wholly his. It was all a matter of grace, and not of keeping the law.

Paul had supposed that the Gentiles were to receive justification in the same way as the Jews, namely, through the observance of the law. But it had now become clear to him that the Jews were to get it in another way,— from the favor and mercy of the Messiah; and it seemed the natural consequence that the heathen should obtain it in the same way, namely, through faith in him. With this conviction that Jesus was the Messiah, whose death was the sin-offering, the law at once fell away. Paul had entirely misunderstood it and its purposes. It now assumed an entirely different character in his eyes. It was this, his conception of the importance and meaning of Christ's death and resurrection, that was *his gospel*. It was not that he differed from the others in the facts which he preached, but in the interpretation of them.

And now began his remarkable career as an itinerant evangelist. With feverish zeal he began his life of wandering, which was interrupted only by his imprisonment and ended by his death, — a life full of toil and suffering, of want and danger, of violence and pain, of " hair-breadth 'scapes by flood and field," glimpses into which are given us especially in his second letter to the Corinthians. "Woe is me if I preach not the gospel" was the sentiment that took overpowering possession of him, and drove him on with unflagging steps. Not that it was a burden to him; on the contrary, it was his meat and drink, his joy and comfort, his very life. So wholly surrendered was he to the Messiah who appeared to him on the way to Damascus, so eager to obey him, to act in accordance with his will and desire, to live for him and labor in his spirit, that it was possible for him to say, " I live no longer, but Christ lives in me," his will and powers and personality were so completely swallowed up and made identical with those of Christ.

Paul remained but a short time at Damascus, but even there he began to preach that Jesus is the Messiah. The call to preach among the heathen was an immediate one (Gal. i. 15-17), and he at once went into Arabia and began his work. The name Arabia was applied to all the territory south of Palestine, and also to that east of the Jordan, almost as far north as Damascus; It was at this time a part of what was called Nabatæa, and was ruled by a king named Aretas. Undoubtedly he spent his time there in preaching Christ. It was not a time of meditation, but of earnest work.[1] With what success he was at-

[1] See chapter vii. p. 206.

tended we do not know. But he returned to Damascus, where, according to the Acts, the Jews tried to take his life. But in 2 Cor. xi. 32, 33, Paul throws a different light on this. He says it was the governor under Aretas that watched the gates in order to seize him. It is not too keen a supposition that Paul met with violent opposition in Arabia and was opposed by Aretas, and had to flee for his life. But the danger did not cease here, for even in Damascus the governor of the city tried to seize him. This is indeed very probable, for there was nothing else so dangerous to a government under which there were many Jews than the proclamation of a Messiah. It was a time in which false Messiahs were numerous, and wherever they appeared they succeeded in winning many followers, and always caused the government a great deal of trouble. The preaching of Paul was that Jesus was the Messiah; and there was nothing that would more quickly cause a commotion than such a message. Just as the Roman governors were fearful of such a movement, so Aretas, who was more familiar with the Jews and their beliefs, thought that this was dangerous to his own position, for he would naturally attach the idea of a temporal rule to the Messiahship of Jesus which Paul was preaching. It is but natural, therefore, that he attempted to seize Paul.

The two accounts contained in 2 Cor. xi. 32, 33, and Acts ix. 23-25, may be harmonized, for we know that everywhere the Jews developed the most bitter hatred against Paul. At any rate they undoubtedly refer to the same event. But Paul escaped the danger by being let down in a basket through an opening in the wall.

The whole story of Aretas and his connection with Paul was for a long time questioned, but without sufficient grounds. For the latest researches have shown that there is really nothing known that can be urged against the truthfulness of the narrative. Aretas IV. was king of Arabia Nabatæa, whose capital was Petrea. His kingdom included a large part of the Sinaitic peninsula, and extended far up on the east side of the Jordan. He was a warlike man, a skillful general, and an able ruler. It is impossible to say just when he got control of Damascus, as we have no exact information about it. But it is a very significant fact that the coins of Damascus from the year 33 A. D. to 63 A. D. do not bear the image of the Roman Emperor. But before 33, and after 63, they again appear bearing the Emperor's likeness. This fact shows conclusively that during this period the city did not owe allegiance directly to the Emperor, but was under some other ruler. So that it is possible that Aretas IV. had control of Damascus during this whole period.[1]

How long Paul was in Arabia it is impossible to say. We know only that three years after his con-

---

[1] See Schürer, i. 609 ff.

version he went up to Jerusalem, and it is probable that this was soon after he escaped from Damascus. The object of his visit, he himself tells us, was to make the acquaintance of Peter. The account of this in Acts x. 26-30 would, if that were all we had in regard to it, lead us to suppose that he remained there a long time, and played an important part in the work of the congregation there. But Paul tells us that he was there only fifteen days, and that he saw none of the disciples except Peter and James the brother of Jesus. His brief stay, therefore, would exclude such an interpretation of the passage in Acts. But it is hardly to be supposed that Paul was idle at this time. He attempted to join himself to the Christians, but they were afraid of him, thinking that he was endeavoring in this way to learn all about them, that he might the more easily cause their arrest. But Barnabas had in some way learned of his conversion and work, and was able to assure the Christians in Jerusalem that he was no longer a persecutor. It is impossible to think that Paul could be silent. His zeal never slumbered, and so here at Jerusalem, in the same place where he had made his reputation as a persecutor, he began to bear witness to Christ. But his activity quickly brought him into danger. Of all men's preaching, that of Paul would be most offensive to the Jews. To them he was a second Balaam, for they had sent him out to destroy the sect of the Nazarenes, but he came back an earnest preacher and defender of the hated doctrines. Of course they were enraged at this, and, with the Jewish violence characteristic of that period of their history, they attempted to kill him. He was able to escape them, and set out for his home in Tarsus. This must have been some time about 37 or 38 A. D.

The next information we have about him is that, about 43 or 44, Barnabas brought him from Tarsus to Antioch to help in spreading the gospel among the heathen there. What was he doing in the mean time? Here are at least five or six years of which we have no account. There is not a word about him in all this time. Is it because he was doing nothing? Many have treated this as if it were a matter of course that Paul went back to Tarsus, sat down and folded his hands, and waited for something to turn up. And the thing that finally did turn up was Barnabas with the request to come to Antioch. But all such have failed to appreciate the true character of Paul. He was preaching, of course, as may be seen from many indications. In the first place, we learn from Acts xv. 23 that there were "brethren of the Gentiles in Antioch, Syria, and *Cilicia*," but nothing is said about how Christianity was carried into Cilicia. But, since Paul was several years there, it is easily explained. Again, when Paul and Barnabas set out on their first missionary journey they went first to Cyprus, which was the home of Barnabas, and then, not to Cilicia, which was Paul's home, but to Asia Minor, landing just west of Cilicia, and made a tour through the provinces that bordered Cilicia. Undoubtedly, therefore, he had already evangelized Cilicia during these years of which we know so little.

Again, Acts xi. 25, it is simply said that Barnabas went to seek for Saul; but why he should have thought of Saul for this place, it is not said. That is also easily explained, for Paul had already become widely known because of his labors. He had already a great reputation, and on this account Barnabas thought he should be brought to this promising field. But we have also what amounts to a positive statement by Paul himself, that he spent these years in the work. In Galatians, when explaining his exact connection and intercourse with the apostles and the church at Jerusalem, he says (i. 22, 23), "And I was still unknown by face unto the churches of Judæa which were in Christ; but they only heard say, He that once persecuted us *now preacheth* the faith of which he once made havoc." And when we take this in connection with the verse which precedes it, we have the fullest proof that he was not idle, but was, during all this time, the same restless, eager evangelist with whom we later become acquainted in the Acts and in his letters.

Of his labors in Antioch we know almost nothing, except that he was there "for a whole year," and that the congregation rapidly increased. It is somewhat difficult to fix the account in Acts

xi. 27–30 and xii. 25. According to this, Agabus, a prophet from Jerusalem, came down to Antioch and foretold "that there should be a great famine over all the world, which came to pass in the days of Claudius." Allowing for the common hyperbole, it may be said that there is no difficulty about this part of the account, for as a matter of fact the reign of Claudius was noted for the great number of local famines that occurred. From 44 to 48 A. D., there was much want and suffering in many parts of the empire. The point of difficulty, however, lies in the fact that it is said that Paul and Barnabas both went to Jerusalem with the contribution, while in Galatians Paul says that fourteen years elapsed between his first and second visits to Jerusalem, and the second visit was undoubtedly the same one that is described in the fifteenth chapter of Acts. A satisfactory explanation of this contradiction has not yet been made.[1]

Again we come to a long period of which we have very little information. The so-called council which is described in Acts xv. must have taken place in the year 50, or early in the year 51. But,

---

[1] Of course, for one who admits that it is possible for the author of the Acts to have made a mistake, the passage presents no difficulty; for such a one would simply say, Luke was misinformed, and hence was wrong in saying that Paul went to Jerusalem with the collection. For it is not to be supposed that Paul was in error when he assured the Galatians that for fourteen years he was not in Judæa, and they knew of him only by hearsay.

by the most liberal reckoning, the year's residence of Paul and Barnabas in Antioch would bring us to the year 44 or 45 at the most. For all this intervening period of five years at least, we have no information except what is contained in the thirteenth and fourteenth chapters. In these we have an account of what is called Paul's first missionary journey, but it is impossible that it should have filled out the whole period. It can hardly have lasted more than a year or two. Besides, we have no means of telling whether this took place early in this period or toward the end of it. This shows how scanty our sources of knowledge about this period are. Of one thing only are we sure, namely, that Paul continued his work, but where and with what success it is impossible to say. It is a curious fact that we have so little information about Paul and his work until after the council at Jerusalem. So much, however, is clear: he was working among the heathen, and laying the foundation for the great Gentile Christian church. He was doing this without any opposition from the Jewish Christians, for they were yet in ignorance of his principles and methods. When they did come with this demand it was too late; Christianity among the heathen, without any of the legal observances, was already a success, so that Paul and his fellow-workers could point with triumph to the Gentile Christian congregations, for the work of grace in them differed in no respect from that among the Jewish Christians.

Although we know so little of these years, yet one thing is certain: Paul was already known and recognized as the apostle to the Gentiles. It was because of this that he had suffered persecution in Damascus. And when he went to Jerusalem to the council, in the year 50, the apostles there admitted that Paul had been intrusted with the gospel to the uncircumcised. That was the reputation which he had already made for himself.

During this time Christianity was firmly established in Antioch, and Paul in accordance with his calling, which was that of a missionary, began to look about for a new field. Under these circumstances the Holy Spirit said, "Separate me Barnabas and Saul for the work whereunto I have called them." It is not necessary, in fact it is wrong, to attribute this to some supernatural and uncommon manifestation. According to the way of thinking and speaking of the early Christians, every good work was inspired by, and done in, the Holy Spirit, and hence was attributed directly to him. And just as every good impulse was referred to the influence or voice of the Holy Spirit, so this beginning of what may be called foreign missions is said to have been made in accordance with his commands.

It is difficult to say what the ceremony of the laying on of hands meant to them. Paul certainly did not regard it as conferring any authority or power on him, for he everywhere repudiates with the greatest vehemence the thought that he was in any way indebted to any one but Christ for his command and authority. According to this, Paul cannot have looked upon it as in any way an *official*, but rather as a symbolic act.

The first verse of the thirteenth chapter contains an interesting notice to the effect that in the church at Antioch there were prophets and teachers, and these in connection with the congregation are represented as sending out the missionaries. It is to be noted that there is nothing said of deacons and presbyters, or bishops.

Barnabas and Paul were ready to set out on their first long journey. They took with them John Mark as their "attendant." It will be remembered that he was a resident of Jerusalem, and that it was to his mother's house that Peter went after escaping from prison. He was a cousin or nephew of Barnabas; which, it is not clear, for the Greek word is indefinite. From the fact that he is called their attendant, many have written about him as if he were their servant, and so they give us an absurd picture of Barnabas and Paul traveling about with a courier to do for them all the services that are required of such a body servant. But the Greek word can with equal propriety be translated "helper," and it is more than once used of Paul himself (see Acts xxvi. 16 and 1 Cor. iv. 1). It would bring them both into the most ridiculous light if they quarreled so about the choice of a courier. It was because he "went not with them to the work" that Paul afterwards refused to take him again, and that expression shows clearly that he was their fellow-missionary, and sustained the same relations to and "attended" them in the same way that Silas and Timothy afterwards did.

Barnabas was himself a native of Cyprus (Acts iv. 36, 37), and that explains why they chose that as their first field of endeavor. But only one event of all their stay in the island is described. It was after they had passed through the whole length of the island and reached Paphos, the residence of the proconsul. Here they came into contact with one of the numerous religious quacks that infested that age.

Cyprus was at this time a senatorial province, and consequently was governed by a proconsul. The governors of the imperial provinces were called propraetors. The governor who was then in the island bore the name of Sergius Paulus, and our author makes of him the complimentary remark that he was "a man of understanding." The compliment was a just one, for he was himself an author and the friend of literary men. Pliny in his work on Natural History, Books II. and XVIII., gives the names of several authors, and among them is the name of this Sergius Paulus. Pliny says that he had written a work about the island of Cyprus.[1] It is said that he "believed," but we have no means of knowing what his after life

---

[1] See Cesnola, *Cyprus*, p. 425, where there is a copy of an inscription which was made by him and in which his name occurs.

was, or how fully he identified himself with Christians. It must be remembered that it was a time when the worship of one God did not exclude that of another.

They sailed from Paphos to the coast of Asia Minor, and after landing came to Perga in Pamphylia, the first province west of Cilicia. It was here that Mark deserted them, returning to his mother in Jerusalem. No direct reason for his conduct is assigned, but it is probable that his Jewish conscience was troubling him, and he was unwilling to associate with the Gentiles. It must be remembered that until recently he had been in Jerusalem. This would certainly explain why Paul was so unwilling to take him with them on a later occasion. But Mark afterward redeemed himself in the eyes of Paul, for we find him again in his company, and Paul speaks of him with praise. Curiously enough, Mark is the only one, so far as we know, who was connected with both Peter and Paul. So far as our information in the New Testament is concerned, he is much more with Paul than with Peter; but in the later tradition his association with Paul is entirely forgotten, and he is called the interpreter of Peter, the substance of whose preaching he is said to have preserved for us in his gospel.

The account of their journey is so sketchy that it scarcely gives us any idea of their work. Everywhere, as was Paul's custom, they went to the synagogues and began their work there, and everywhere they met with much the same success. Some of the Jews believed, but the majority opposed them with great bitterness and violence. These accused them before the magistrates, stirred up the leading citizens, and, as the surest way of attaining their object, raised a mob either to drive them out or kill them. As the author uses only general and indefinite expressions of time, it is impossible to tell how long they remained in the various places mentioned.

The first Sabbath in Antioch they went into the synagogue. After the reading of the scriptures which formed a regular part of the service in the synagogue, as they were strangers they were asked to speak, if they had any word of exhortation for the people. It was a strange message that they brought, and it is not surprising that they were so eagerly listened to by the multitudes. But their work was not confined wholly to the cities, for the "word of the Lord was spread throughout all the region." But Jewish opposition drove them on, and they came to Iconium,[1] where the same scenes were repeated. However, their success here was more unequivocal, for "a great multitude both of Jews and of Greeks believed."

Again stress of circumstances compelled them to move on and they came to Lystra. Then follows

---

[1] The scene of *Paul and Thecla*, which has already been mentioned, is laid in Iconium. It is probably based on fact, and perhaps contains some historical reminiscences, though much of it is legendary in character.

a narrative that is especially interesting, for it shows how widely the Greek religion and influence were spread. These were Barbarians, not Greeks, and lived in a backwoods province. But they had the Greek religion. They had a temple of Zeus, and their gods all have Greek names. The national gods had been crowded out, and they did not think of them, but spoke of the Greek gods. It shows, too, the difference between that age and this. Their naïve, primitive way of thinking about things has entirely disappeared. It was reported that a lame man had been healed, and they at once said, "The gods have come down to us in the likeness of men." It is hardly necessary to say that in this age this is not the conclusion that would be drawn from such an occurrence. In fact the whole account of this journey shows a primitive population; they believed more easily than others.

The Jews of these cities were thoroughly enraged, and Paul as the principal preacher was of course the principal offender. In their eyes he was guilty of apostasy and sacrilege, and deserving of death. He was seized by a mob, dragged out of the city, stoned, and left for dead. This is confirmed by Paul himself in his second letter to the Corinthians: "Once was I stoned" (xi. 25). How seriously he was injured it is impossible to tell; we know only that he recovered and withdrew to Lystra. After preaching there for some time, they returned apparently by the same route, exhorting and strengthening the disciples they had made. From the port of Attalia they sailed back to Antioch, and there " rehearsed all things that God had done with them, and how that He had opened a door of faith unto the Gentiles."

These two chapters show that the Jewish bonds were completely broken. That was now an accomplished fact, for the heathen had been admitted in great numbers. Missionary work had been carried on among them on a large scale. The question now beginning to press was, How will the Jewish Christians and especially the church at Jerusalem regard these Gentile Christians? Will they receive them as brethren and equals? How will they treat each other? On what plane will they meet? Or will they refuse to unite and each go its own way? Must there be two gospels? Or were there already two gospels, one of the Jewish Christians and one of the Gentiles? It all depended on this one question: " Is the law still binding on those who believe in Christ?"

CHAPTER VI.

THE BURNING QUESTION.

It is necessary in this connection again to call attention to the fact that the Jewish Christians, especially the members of the Mother Church at Jerusalem, were still observing the law. They had not broken with Judaism, and it had not entered their thoughts that their Christianity could exist apart from the observance of the Jewish law. They were zealous for the law and regarded it as essential to Christianity. Stephen had got a better insight into the new dispensation, but the promulgation of his views had cost him his life. Only Peter had preached to the heathen, and he but once. The group that had gathered in the house of Cornelius to hear him was the only heathen audience that he had faced, and his success there had been a surprise to him. But the Christians at Jerusalem had rebuked him for associating with the uncircumcised. That this was the attitude of the church at Jerusalem there can be no doubt. It is evident that here was a difference between them and Paul, and all who, like him, preached to the heathen without requiring them to keep the law.

That we may see just what this difference was

let us sum up in a few sentences the principal truths which formed the substance of what was preached by them all. What was the common faith? What were the principal truths of their message?[1]

They have already been given, but it will be well to repeat them briefly. They all began with the declaration that Jesus is the Messiah, and endeavored to prove this from the writings of the Old Testament. It was all interpreted in such a way as to make it refer to him with little or no regard to its original meaning. They all agreed in recounting the principal events of his life. Especially, however, is this true of his death and resurrection. He had begun a kingdom which was now in process of building, and he would soon return to establish it perfectly. That this formed a part of the common belief ought to be beyond all question. Paul speaks of it frequently, and it occurs in almost every writing of the New Testament. It is not meant that they all thought of this kingdom in the same way, or that they agreed as to its form, or even that they had a fixed idea about it. For they spoke of it in such figurative apocalyptic language that it is impossible to get a clear idea in all respects of just what they expected. But the fact remains the same that they all expected that Christ would come again, although they were perhaps not agreed as to what would happen in connection with his coming.

[1] For this, see the epoch-making work of Prof. Harnack, *Dogmengeschichte*, i. 30-270.

They all agreed, too, in declaring that sins were forgiven and grace and favor with God were to be had through him. Christ himself, in the mysterious words, "This is my body which is given for you," undoubtedly connected the forgiveness of sins with his own death, and this certainly formed a prominent part of the preaching of the early disciples. And they all proclaimed that the Holy Spirit was the common possession of all who believed in Christ. He was not given to a few in such measure that they were the controlling element, but in the matter of authority they were all on the same plane, for all possessed the Holy Spirit.

There was complete agreement on all these principal points among the Christians of all parties. Where was the difference, then? It lay in the answers given to the question, What is necessary to secure salvation? or, as it was formulated by them, On what condition can one have a share in the Messiah's kingdom?

The common view among the Jews was that a man's salvation depended on whether he kept the law or not. The faithful son of Abraham was the one who obeyed and observed all those commands, and he alone might claim all that God had in store for his people, and he alone was assured that in the Messiah's kingdom there was a place of honor reserved for him.

But now a new condition had been added, for they all declared, "Believe in the Lord Jesus

Christ and thou shalt be saved." Faith in him, that is, the confidence that he was the Messiah and officially represented God, and that he would graciously receive as members of his kingdom all who would repent and call upon him, was all that was required as the new condition of salvation. It was the relation between these two conditions that now had to be determined. Were they to be coördinated? Were both to be equally binding? Or was one of them to be regarded as more important than the other? Which then should have the precedence? Or was the new entirely to displace the old?

There were at least three, possibly four, answers given to this question almost from the first. The one was that of the so-called Judaizing Christians. We know from Acts xv. and Galatians, as well as from other scattered notices in other letters of Paul, that these declared that without the observance of the law there was no salvation. They insisted that all heathen who believe in Christ should be circumcised, celebrate all the feasts, and keep the Mosaic law as it had been required of the Jews. According to them this was absolutely necessary for salvation. Judaism is the only door into Christianity, which is the perfected, completed Judaism. In favor of this view they could urge that the Messiah himself had lived as a Jew in subjection to the law. What higher proof of its holiness could be demanded? There were many of these who were filled with zeal for the introduction of the law among the heathen, and labored with never-failing energy in the accomplishment of this. They declared that all who did not observe the law were still in their sins, no matter how great their faith in the Messiah.

The second answer to the question was that the Jewish Christians must keep the law. It was looked upon as a part of the national religious inheritance of the Jews, to disregard which was an act of treason to the nation. The peculiar prerogative and higher rank of the Jews in the Messiah's kingdom were assured just because of their observance of this law. The heathen were to be admitted to this kingdom, but they were to be inferior to the Jews. The nobility of this new kingdom was to be composed of those that had kept the law. The passage Acts xxi. 20 is decisive on this point. It is worth quoting again. " Thou seest, brother, how many thousands there are among the Jews of them which have believed; and they are all zealous for the law: and they have been informed concerning thee, that thou teachest all the Jews which are among the Gentiles to forsake Moses, telling them not to circumcise their children, neither to walk after the customs." Look at this carefully and see just what the charge against Paul is. What was it that made James fear that the Jewish Christians in Jerusalem would do violence to Paul? Was it that he was preaching the gospel to the Gentiles without requiring them to keep the law? That is not what the passage says. It was because he was teaching the "*Jews* which are among the Gentiles to forsake Moses, telling them not to circumcise their children, neither to walk after the customs." That is, for the Jew the law was still holy and binding, and simple faith in Jesus as the Messiah was not sufficient. This was undoubtedly the opinion of a large majority of the Jewish Christians. But what was their attitude to the Gentiles who believed in Jesus? They admit that such could have part in the Messiah's kingdom, but they were on a lower plane. They recognized them as Christians, but if they did not keep the law they could not associate with them. The old levitical distinctions of clean and unclean were still in force. These views were in themselves contradictory, but the contradiction was not felt by the Jews. At Antioch (Gal. ii.), for example, those from James and Peter and Barnabas and the others did not deny that the heathen members were Christians, but only claimed that they themselves, by their observance of the law, were placed on a higher plane of holiness, which excluded their free association and intercourse.

The third answer was that of Paul, which needs hardly be stated, for through the work of the Reformers of the sixteenth century it has come to be the watchword of Protestantism. Faith in Christ is the only condition of salvation. The law is done away with, it has its end in Christ. This formed an integral part of his Gospel, and he has defended it with great skill and power in his two letters to the Galatians and Romans.

But what was Paul's attitude to the law? He had once thought that its observance was the *only* way of salvation, now he sees that it *never* was the way of salvation. Its purpose was not to save. Nevertheless for Paul the law was divine, it was God's word. But the promise was older than the law, for long before it was given to Moses God had made the promise to Abraham, and the great blessing was connected with the promise and not with the keeping of the law. For Abraham had not kept the law, but simply believed God. In this Paul sees the original purpose of God, which was to give the blessing to those who believe. Promise is primary and fundamental in God's dealings with and relations to man. The law came in between the promise and its fulfillment, but it could not in any way invalidate the promise, for God had not only promised, He had solemnly given an oath that the promise should be fulfilled. The law, then, coming in between the promise and its fulfillment, could be binding only until the promise should be fulfilled, and this was done in the coming of the Messiah. The law is medial and temporary. It formed a part of God's plan and had a special purpose. This purpose is expressed by Paul in various ways, the most general of which is that it was to teach that sin is sinful, or to show what sin is.

It does this in several ways. In the first place,

it reveals the character of God and shows that He hates sin. And it shows what is sinful by forbidding it. The "Thou shalt not" of itself shows that it is sinful and that God can have no pleasure in it. From the character of the things that are forbidden and commanded in the law, one should be able to form a proper idea of the character of God and of the nature of sin. But the law had still another purpose. It said, "Do this," but in spite of the command there was no one that was able to say that he had obeyed. It said, "Do not do this," but who was there that had refrained? When brought face to face with the law there was no one who was clear, but all were convicted of sin. It was impossible not to feel the burden of sin resting on the soul, for all had been disobedient. All felt that there was need of mercy, but who could be sure that God would be merciful? The law, then, was to lead men to Christ, by awakening in them the consciousness of sin, the desire to know that God is merciful, and so put them into such a state that they would gladly receive the gospel of Jesus, which was that God is the Father of all, and like a father pitieth his children, is long-suffering, gracious, merciful, and freely forgives all who repent and call upon Him. That was the good news which Christ proclaimed to the world, but, that it might be accepted, it was necessary that there should be present the sense of sin and estrangement from God.

And now that Christ is come the law is no longer

binding; it is done away, it has its end in Christ. But what does that mean? How is it that Christ is the end of the law? How could he " fulfill " the law? To this question we have not only Paul's answer, we have also that of Christ, and they entirely agree.

In the minds of those who heard Christ there had arisen the question, what is the attitude of this man to the law? It seemed to them that he was going to break entirely away from the law and the prophets and begin on a new foundation. They thought that he was beginning a new religion on new and different principles, disregarding completely all the religious truth that they already possessed. It was in answer to these, their thoughts, that Jesus used the words, " Think not that I came to destroy the law or the prophets : I came not to destroy but to fulfill " (Matt. v. 17). The word " fulfill " is a misleading translation, for it seems to say that Christ came to keep the law, to observe it, to obey its commands. And so it is often interpreted as if it meant that in this way Christ had fulfilled the law for us : because he was circumcised, he was circumcised for us ; because he kept the feasts and fasts and observed all the levitical distinctions, he did it for us, and we are therefore free from all this. In that he kept God's law perfectly he kept it for us, and his observance of it is imputed to us. But " fulfill " here has an entirely different meaning. It means to fill up, to fill out, to complete, to accomplish perfectly what it could only imperfectly do. That is, Christ says that he came to carry on the work of the law until its purpose should be entirely accomplished. And so Christ proceeds, and a large part of the Sermon on the Mount is simply the filling out, the completing, of the teaching of the law. He begins with the warning, "Unless your righteousness is better than that of the scribes and Pharisees ye shall in no wise enter into the kingdom of heaven." But these were the very people that were keeping the law so carefully! What was the matter then? They put their righteousness in the observance of the single commands of the law, as if that was the important thing. The condition of the heart was for them a matter of indifference. But Christ by a few practical examples shows what he means by "fulfilling" the law. The command was, "Thou shalt not kill," and the Jew thought if he had not actually taken the life of any one he had kept the law. Christ shows how superficial is such a conception of the sin of murder. Not only the act of murder, but every angry, violent word, even every unspoken, angry feeling and thought of the heart, is murder. That is a deepening of the teaching of the law. In the same way Christ "fulfills" the teaching of the law in regard to adultery. This consists not simply in the performance of the act, but every lustful thought is adultery. And so in regard to oaths, almsgiving, prayer, fasting, and other things. In all these Christ is showing that evil and good are of the heart, not of the external action. In this he was filling up and perfecting the teaching of the law and the prophets. He was deepening the knowledge of sin and its character. In this respect he takes up the work of the law and completes it. He shows that it is not the single commands of the law that have such importance, but the whole law in its purpose to make known the character of God and the nature of sin.

What was the life and work of Christ but the revelation of God? How patiently and persistently he strove to teach his disciples the true character of God. He was the revealer and image of the Father, in that in his love for sinners, in his willingness to forgive them, in his desire to save them, he was but showing them that that was the way in which God looked upon them; that that was God's attitude toward them. And this is the principal truth in the Christian religion, that in Christ we have the sure knowledge of the character of God and the assurance that He is gracious and that Christ's attitude to sinners is the same as that of God himself.

And now as Christ takes up this work, completing and perfecting it, and accomplishing it so much better than the law itself possibly could, the law is no longer necessary; it has served its purpose, and hence is laid aside. On the principle that the higher always supersedes the lower, Christ supersedes it, and hence he is the end of the law.

The original promise now has its full force.

Abraham was blessed simply by believing God, by faith, so now the blessing which Christ brought, and all his benefits, all that he has to give, are to be got in the same way, by believing him.

But this would apply to the Jews who had the law; what about the heathen who were not the descendants of Abraham and who were without the law? They did not have the law, but they had something parallel to it, namely, the conscience; and this served the same purpose among the heathen as the law among the Jews. It was not so efficient, but even the heathen through the action of their conscience knew that there is a holy God, that they had sinned against Him and needed forgiveness. The conscience told them that they needed salvation, but it could not save them. Neither the law nor the conscience ever saved any one, that was not their purpose. Salvation is the free gift of God to those that believe Him.

It should be noted that in the first chapters of the letter to the Romans Paul is not discussing the question whether any of the heathen are saved or not, any more than whether any of the Jews are saved. But he is showing that God had not left himself without witness, having given the Jews the law and the heathen conscience. By this, all the world was made conscious of sin. If any of the Jews were saved, they had been saved as Abraham was, through faith in God. In like manner, if any of the heathen were saved (and Paul certainly admits the possibility of this, see Romans

ii. 6-16 and 26-29), they were saved, not by their conscience, not through their knowledge of any particular dogma, but because in their hearts they felt the burden of sin, and were truly penitent, and believed that God would be gracious to them. It all depended on the attitude of their hearts toward God, and not on their exact knowledge nor on their living up to the light which they had. It cannot be too often said that religion does not consist in knowledge about God, nor in a creed that can be repeated, nor in the punctual observance of any law or laws, but it is of the heart. "A broken and a contrite heart, O God, thou wilt not despise." That of course put Jew and Gentile on the same plane. There is no longer any difference between them, for both may believe God.

But strangely enough none of these three answers was the one that finally prevailed in the church during the first centuries. The Judaizers failed in their attempt to make the law binding on all. They caused great trouble in the church for several years, but it was impossible for them to succeed. The Jewish Christians gave up the law, apparently very soon after the destruction of the temple (70 A. D.), and probably under the impression which this event made on them, that God had thereby deserted the people that had been unfaithful to Him. But even Paul's answer was not the one that was generally understood and accepted in the church, but in its stead another, which was much easier to understand. It was as follows: the law is still binding, but it was never intended to be understood literally. Even from the first God had not intended that the commands should be interpreted according to the law, but their true meaning was to be found by allegorizing them. For instance, God had forbidden the Jews to eat the flesh of birds of prey. But what did this mean? Simply that they were not to live as birds of prey, that get their living by robbery, theft, and violence. The command not to eat flesh of swine meant that they should not be like swine, filthy in character, and associate with such. The command not to eat the flesh of the hare meant that they were not to be adulterous, for the hare was the symbol of adultery. In this way the whole Old Testament could still be held and made binding, but a "deeper sense" was obtained from it. Thousands of Jews in the first centuries became Christians and justified their non-observance of the law in this way. The Christians really got rid of the law in this way, and not as Paul did.

Paul's explanation did not become popular and prevail for several reasons: 1. The allegorical method was in vogue. Everything was treated in this way, and it must be said that it is a very simple way of cutting the Gordian knot. The uneducated could easily understand it, while Paul's reasoning was fine and difficult to comprehend; 2. Besides, Paul himself did not consistently follow out his position to its logical consequences. He declared plainly that the law and the prophets belonged to the past, the old dispensation was succeeded by the new; Christ had put everything on a new basis, because he had brought a higher, more complete revelation. It followed from this that the Old Testament should be subordinated to this revelation which Christ brought. It really could no longer be an absolute authority for the Christian, for, for him, Christ alone could be that. Paul used the word law in several senses. Sometimes it was the Mosaic law, sometimes the levitical law, sometimes the combined teachings of the whole Old Testament, sometimes the moral law was included, sometimes excluded. Sometimes he declared the whole law, the whole old dispensation, was done away; not even the law about the Sabbath was binding (Col. ii. 16), but all things were become new in Christ, and subject only to his will. And yet he quoted the Old Testament to prove the Messiahship of Christ and made a pedagogical use of it which showed that it still had a certain authority in his eyes.

3. And then Paul himself prepared the way for the entrance of this allegorizing method. In fact, he used the allegorical method himself, in certain passages, to get rid of the letter of the law. It is necessary to refer only to the letter to the Romans (ii. 28–30): "For he is not a Jew which is one outwardly; neither is that circumcision which is outward, in the flesh: but he is a Jew which is one inwardly, and circumcision is that of the heart, in the spirit, not in the letter."

In other words, Paul really solved this problem in two ways: by his fine method of reasoning as shown above, which was so difficult to understand, and if followed out would do away with the whole Old Testament, and by the allegorical method, which was familiar to all and easily comprehended.[1]

4. The Old Testament, in spite of Paul's statement that it was superseded by the revelation of Christ, lived on in the church principally because, in the first place, it was regarded as a revelation from God, and in the second place, it was the arsenal, the source of weapons against the Jews. In the second century there was an attempt made to rise to Paul's position in regard to the Old Testament, but coupled with it such a false estimate of it and of its origin that it could not succeed. And so Paul's fundamental position in regard to the Old Testament has never yet been properly studied and recognized; but theoretically every part of the Old Testament is put on the same plane with the words of Jesus, the genealogies of the Chronicles stand side by side with the Sermon on the Mount. But this can be justified only by the allegorical method of interpretation and a false conception of Jewish history.

The first intimation that we have that the trouble about the observance of the law was be-

---

[1] See also Phil. iii. 3, where Paul claims that those who believe in Christ are the true circumcision. It was a common thought among the Christians that they were the true seed of Abraham. See also his use of allegory in Gal. iv. 21–31.

coming acute is in the fifteenth chapter of Acts. This must have been about the year 49 A. D. "And certain men came down from Judæa and taught the brethren, saying, Except ye be circumcised after the custom of Moses, ye cannot be saved" (xv. 1). These were the "Judaizers."[1] They were Christians, they believed in the Messiahship of Jesus, but they held to the law at the same time, and insisted that it must be observed by all who would become members of his kingdom. This declaration raised a great commotion among the Gentile Christians in Antioch. Some of them had for years been watching with great joy and confident expectation for the return of Christ. We can easily imagine their consternation when they were told that they would certainly be excluded from his kingdom if they did not also keep the law. All their hopes were blasted. But Paul and Barnabas vigorously defended themselves and their teaching. The struggle was a serious one, and it must have shaken the church to its very foundation, for there was "no small dissension and questioning with them" about this important matter.

The mission among the heathen had been successful beyond all question. Paul was not the only one that had been communicating the gospel to them. They now formed a large minority in the whole church. The time had now come when the

[1] That is, as their name indicates, they wished to make others live as the Jews, according to the Jewish law, to "Judaize."

Mother Church at Jerusalem must recognize this. So Paul and Barnabas went to Jerusalem to lay the matter before them and compel the recognition of their work. We have two accounts of this meeting in Jerusalem, the one in Acts xv., the other in Gal. ii., so by comparing and uniting these we may get a good idea of what took place at that time.

In the first place it is clear that Paul and Barnabas and Titus and perhaps others went up to Jerusalem. It was a matter of some practical importance for Paul that he could take with him one of his disciples, a Gentile, as a sample of his workmanship. He could show them in the person of Titus what Christianity could do without any help of the law. The "Acts of the Apostles" generally represents Paul as working under the direction of the church at Antioch, while Paul in all his letters declares that he is directly under the command of Christ. It is characteristic therefore of the Acts that it says that the church at Antioch *appointed* these to go to Jerusalem, while Paul in Galatians says that they went up *by revelation*. The two accounts are not necessarily in contradiction. The manner of the appointment may be so understood that it does not conflict with the freedom and independence of Paul's action. In the Acts we have an account only of the public meetings. Paul and Barnabas met with the whole church, in which James appears as the leading spirit, while Peter appears in a subordinate rôle. The matter was discussed apparently in the presence of the whole congregation, while in the letter to the Galatians Paul seems to say that the whole thing was discussed and settled privately between the pillar Apostles and himself and Barnabas. But if we look carefully at the latter account we find that the public meeting is at least implied, if not directly mentioned. Paul says, " I went up again to Jerusalem ... and I laid before *them* (that is, the brethren at Jerusalem) the gospel which I preached among the Gentiles, and *especially before them* who were of repute" (Gal. ii. 1-2).[1] In the clause "and I laid before *them*" there is therefore a reference to the public meeting which is mentioned in Acts.

There were two parties standing strongly opposed to each other. On the one hand the Judaizers, the "certain of the sect of the Pharisees who believed," demanding that the heathen be circumcised and the whole law be made binding on them. These were Christians, but Paul in his bitterness calls them "false brethren." But it by no means follows that they were not acting with the best motives. They thought that Paul was wrong and they were laboring in every way to overcome him. The other party was composed of Paul and his

[1] The expression κατ' ἰδίαν δὲ can with equal propriety be translated "and especially," as well as "but privately" as in the Revised Version. In fact the thought of the passage requires it to be so translated. The emphasis is put on the fact that the *apostles* in Jerusalem had recognized Paul as having the true gospel.

friends, who declared that the law was not necessary, that faith in Christ was sufficient, and therefore the Gentiles were to be freed from its burdensome regulations. There is something peculiar about the speech of Peter. It is impossible not to feel that there is a kind of exultant tone in it. It sounds very much like the "I told you so" of a man who has been long opposed and has suddenly found a strong reinforcement, which, it seems, is about to bring every one to recognize that he has been in the right. "You know very well," he says, "that long ago, God showed through me that the Gentiles were to have a share in the gospel, and that God gave the Holy Spirit to them as to us; but you refused to recognize that fact, you opposed me then and are still opposing the truth, in the face of all the reports which we have heard from Paul of the work of grace among the Gentiles. You are still tempting God, refusing to follow his plain teaching." It is evident that Peter had been somewhat oppressed by his Judaistic surroundings. He knew that the law was not necessary; his experience with Cornelius had taught him that; but because of the opposition which he had met in Jerusalem he had held himself back, and in order not to break with them, and for the sake of peace, he had not continued the work among the Gentiles. It is a relief to him now to give utterance to these sentiments; it is as if a burden had been rolled off his heart. Theoretically he stood with Paul and Barnabas, but practically with the others, because he had deferred to their opinions. He was willing to give the Gentile Christians the fullest recognition and regard them as brethren. From the gospels and from the later occurrence at Antioch (Gal. ii.) we know that this was wholly in accordance with his character.

But in regard to James the case is somewhat different. From his letter and from the whole tradition that he left behind him, James must have been thoroughly Jewish. He does not wish to oppose God, who is visiting "the Gentiles to take out of them a people for his name." It is clear to James that God is moving upon the Gentiles. He is not confining himself to the Jews alone. But the outcome of this is not yet clear to him. He does not see how the Gentiles are to be brought into connection with God's special people. He takes much the same position as Gamaliel did in regard to the young and rising sect. So James was of the opinion that they should not trouble the Gentiles that are turning to God, but the whole thing should be allowed to take its course. God would conduct it to the proper end. He represents a middle party, then, which was willing to recognize the Gentiles as Christians, but for the present were suspending judgment and were watching for further developments before the two nationalities could be completely united. For James, as we shall soon see, still did not think that the Jewish and Gentile Christians could associate on equal terms. In other words, they were recognized as standing in a true relationship to the Messiah; they were Christians; God was choosing them as his people from among the Gentiles. But the relation between the people He is choosing, the Gentile Christians, and the people He has already chosen, the Jewish Christians, is not yet clear. For the present they must remain sharply divided.

What then was the question that was before them for discussion? Unless we look squarely at this and get it fixed, we are likely to make many false inferences. The question was a simple and single one, namely: must the Gentiles keep the law in order to have a part in the Messiah and his kingdom? There is not a word said about whether the Jews should keep it or not; that was taken for granted: at any rate it was not discussed. The whole attention of the meeting was taken up with the Gentile Christians and the law. "But there rose up certain of the sect of the Pharisees who believed, saying, it is needful to circumcise them and to charge them to keep the law of Moses." These demanded that Titus should be circumcised. There was a sharp struggle about this, but Paul carried his point. Gentile Christianity was on trial in the person of Titus. The examination was satisfactory and Titus was not circumcised.

We come now to the decisions reached. To what agreements did they come? What was the result of all this discussion?

The first and most important one was that the law is not binding on the Gentile Christians. In this Paul was completely victorious. It was this principle for the recognition of which he was laboring, and it was here fully conceded. James, Peter, and John recognized that Paul and Barnabas were true preachers of the true gospel. They had been intrusted with the gospel to the Gentiles, and God had recognized their work by blessing it with success. For their preaching among the heathen had been attended with the same signs and results as that of the other apostles among the Jews.

The second decision was to the effect that this gospel of Paul was for the heathen alone and not for the Jews (Gal. ii. 9). Paul might preach to the Gentiles without demanding of them the observance of the law, but that was not the gospel for the Jews. He might preach to the Jews, but he must not teach them to disregard the law of Moses. In other words, they divided the mission field according to nationality. They thereby laid the possible foundation for two great churches, for two organizations, the one Jewish, the other Gentile, sharply divided and opposing each other, much as Protestantism and Roman Catholicism oppose each other to-day. The very fact that they desired that Paul preach his gospel only to the heathen, and they their gospel to the Jews, shows that they expected Christianity to be thus divided, that they regarded the law as binding on the Jews, and that there could be no union, no free, familiar intercourse on an equal footing between the two nationalities.

The third decision was a peculiar one, for it was based on the belief, in which even Paul shared, that in spite of the freedom of the gospel and the right of the Gentiles to a share in it, the Jews were nevertheless possessed of a special prerogative; that they occupied in some respects the place of honor. They demanded that Paul remember the poor, that is, that he should cause his heathen converts to contribute to the support of the poor Christians among the Jews, and especially of those in Jerusalem. This Paul was willing to do, for it was entirely in accordance with his ideas about the peculiar prerogative of the Jews. In the letter to the Romans (iii. 1 ff.) Paul asks, what advantage has the Jew over the Greek, if both are now to be admitted to the Messiah's kingdom in the same way and on equal terms? And he himself gives the answer. First, it was a great honor for the Jews that they had been intrusted with the oracles of God. Through them the whole world had been blessed, for through them God had made known to the world far more religious truth than through any other people. In this they had been the chosen people of God, and that was a great honor for them. A special promise had been made to them as a people, that they should be a blessing to the whole world. And then the Messiah had come from them; he was a Jew, which was also an honor for them. Paul also expresses the same truth a little differently in the same letter, xv. 27, "For if the Gentiles have been made partakers of their spiritual things, they owe it to them also to minister to them in carnal things." The Jews had been the bearers of religious truth to the Gentiles and rightly deserved to have a share in their wealth. The same thought of the special prerogative of the Jew over the Gentile is also expressed in Rom. i. 16 and elsewhere; "For the gospel is the power of God unto salvation to every one that believeth, *to the Jew first*, and also to the Greek." And it was in accordance with this that Paul always began his work by going to the Jews first, for he believed that they had a special right to the first offer of the gospel. This may be regarded by some as an inconsistency in Paul.

In all this Paul had made no concession in any way. His apostleship and gospel had been recognized and it had been admitted that the law in general, and circumcision in particular, were not to be demanded of the Gentile Christians. He had won his cause, he had been justified in everything. The heathen were free from any and every observance of the demands of the Old Testament. This principle was fixed. Nevertheless, for the sake of the Jews who could not be brought to understand and accept this, for whom Moses was still an authority, the Gentile Christians were asked to abstain from certain things which were most offensive to the Jews. The request was based on the principle of brotherly love. They were not bound to do this, but it was that they might avoid giving offense to weaker brethren. It was not a compromise of the principle for which Paul had so determinedly contended. But it was in accordance with his other principle to which he often gave expression, as in 1 Cor. viii. 13, "If meat maketh my brother to stumble I will eat no flesh forevermore, that I make not my brother to stumble."

In accordance with this, they were asked to abstain from the pollution of idols, which is otherwise expressed in xv. 29, as "things sacrificed to idols;" that is, they were not to eat anything that had been offered in the temples, or been used in connection with the heathen worship. A few years later this same question was raised in Corinth, and Paul gave them the same answer. He told them that this in and of itself was not wrong, but they should refrain from it because of the weaker brethren who would thereby be offended. They were further to keep themselves from fornication, and this is here to be taken in the widest sense of the word, according to which it included not only fornication and adultery, but probably also marriage between persons who were nearly related. It was probably meant therefore to forbid the marriages that are forbidden in Lev. xviii. It must be said also that the heathen are apt to look upon lust as a natural appetite, which could be satisfied as innocently as that of hunger or thirst. They were further asked to have regard to the feelings of the Jews in the use of blood. They were fond of flesh from which the blood had not been extracted, and even drank blood mingled with wine. In order to preserve the blood in the flesh it was the custom to strangle the animals. For the Jew this was an offense, because, according to his conceptions, the blood was the seat of the soul, that is, of the life.[1] Paul agreed to this, not as necessary and legally binding, but because it was all based on the principle of Christian brotherly love. It was not a yielding of the great principle of the freedom of the Gospel.

The purpose of this was simply that the Jews might not be offended; it did not look toward the complete union of the Gentile and Jewish Christians. It was not intended that if the Gentiles should observe these things the Jews should associate with them. For the observance of these was not sufficient on the part of the Gentiles to have free, untrammeled intercourse with them. They were still only " God fearing," they were not proselytes. And so here the question of association was not discussed, and that cannot have been the purpose of these concessions. That was a question for the future. It came up not long after this at Antioch (Gal. ii. 11 ff.). It may have been broached, but it certainly was not settled at this time in Jerusalem. There were at any rate differences of opinion among the leaders in regard to this. Paul had already settled it for himself, and

[1] See Gen. ix. 6, Lev. iii. 17, vii. 26, xvii. 10-24 and elsewhere.

was associating freely with the Gentiles. Peter had theoretically come to the same principle, but because of his surroundings had not practiced it. But James was still of the opinion that they could not associate. For him, the distinctions of clean and unclean according to the levitical law were still in force. We cannot but look upon this as an inconsistency and weakness in James. He did not fully comprehend the nature of Christianity and of religion in general, since he attributed to certain actions a religious worth in and of themselves, while Christ had said that the religious worth of everything depends on the heart. James had in common with his Pharisaic cotemporaries this trait of "externality in religion."

That these concessions were not intended to make free intercourse and complete union of the two nationalities possible is clear from two facts. In the first place, the mission field was divided; Paul was to preach his gospel only to the Gentiles and the others were to preach to the Jews. What sense can there be in such a division, if Jews and Gentiles were to associate freely and all legal and national distinctions were to be disregarded? That can only mean that in the church Jews and Gentiles were to be sharply separated each from the other, and the thing that separated them was the observance of the law.

The second fact is the conduct of Peter in Antioch, not long after this meeting at Jerusalem, an account of which is contained in Gal. ii. Peter had come to Antioch, and there in accordance with his real convictions began to associate with the Gentile members of the church without any regard to levitical distinctions. He was simply following what he had long known to be the truth, but because of the opposition from those about him had not put into practice. But here at Antioch the liberal party was in the majority; for them the question was already settled, and Peter showed by his conduct that he wholly agreed with Paul. But now mark what happened. "Certain came from James," and out of fear Peter drew back from his Gentile friends because he feared "them of the circumcision." That throws a peculiar light on Peter's life from the time of the conversion of Cornelius. He had lost caste with the majority of the church at Jerusalem at that time by associating with the uncircumcised. And it is to be noted that from that time on he no longer holds the first place in Jerusalem, but James, who was far more strict than he, now takes the leading position in the church at Jerusalem. Peter had thereby lost the leadership because of his attitude to the Gentiles. But he had not gone on and, in spite of the opposition, developed an independent activity, but had yielded to the pressure and confined his work to the Jews. And now when "these came from James," he must have known whether they actually represented the opinion of James or not. He did not wish to expose himself to further rebukes from that party, and so he withdrew himself from the association with the Gentiles; and that not openly and at once, but in such a way as to seem to be still associating with them. He was between two fires: on the one hand he wished not to offend the strict party, and on the other he did not wish to act contrary to his better knowledge and offend the Gentiles. Out of his strong desire to be at peace with all, he was led to try to appear to be on both sides of the fence at once. He did not wish to come into further disrepute with the Jewish Christians, especially with those at Jerusalem.

This yielding to those who he knew were in the wrong, and acting contrary to his own convictions, was in Paul's eyes hypocrisy, though it by no means follows that Peter felt that he was guilty of such a sin. Paul thought that the principle of freedom was attacked and the peace of mind of the Gentiles disturbed. For this Paul probably rebuked him. Unfortunately we do not know what Peter said in excuse of his conduct, but it is clear that in principle he agreed with Paul, and that he had yielded only in the belief that he would thereby avoid unpleasant relations with James and his strict party at Jerusalem.

For the sake of clearness let us recapitulate. There were therefore at this time among the Christians three opinions in regard to the law. The first, it is binding on all and is to be understood literally; the second, it is binding only on the Jews, but the Gentiles and Christians who do not observe it are on a lower plane, and may not associate with those who do keep it; the third, it is binding on none; it has done its work in the religious education of the Jews and is now superseded by the higher dispensation. A fourth appeared a few years later and finally prevailed over all the others, that it is binding on all, but is to be understood allegorically. The representatives of the second and third opinions were agreed in this, namely, that the Gentiles need not keep the law; but they differed in the conclusions which they drew from it. The one party failed to see that it necessarily followed from such an admission that the Jews and Gentiles might freely associate with each other, while for Paul that was the only logical inference that could be drawn from it. The council at Jerusalem recognized that the Gentiles were Christians although they did not observe the law; but out of regard to the prejudices or the weakness of the Jews they were asked to observe certain regulations which, however, were not to be regarded as sufficient to allow free and untrammeled intercourse and association between them. On the contrary, they were to be separated from each other, each party following its own principles and development. There existed then a Jewish Christian division and a Gentile Christian division, and there was danger that the two would go farther and farther apart, and that Christianity would thus from the first be divided into two great sects.

It is apparent then that in this council neither

party got everything it desired. Concessions were made, although on the Christian principle of brotherly love. But the council was a failure in many respects. The Judaizers were not at all satisfied with it, and refused to be bound by it. From this time on they increased in bitterness toward Paul, and developed greater hostility and activity against him and his work. From 50 to 70, and perhaps a little later, they continued to labor to compel the Gentiles to observe the law. The end of the struggle is lost to our sight because we have no literature from that period, but we can be sure from various arguments that it lasted until the Fall of Jerusalem. It ended in a half victory and half defeat for both parties. For, contrary to Paul, the church came to believe that the law is binding on all; but contrary to the Judaizers, that it is not to be understood literally but allegorically.

The council failed to bring James and the Gentile Christians any nearer together. He still remained attached to the law, and there is nothing to show that he ever yielded from this position, but he always regarded even the Gentile Christians as ceremonially unclean, and therefore unable to associate with the Jews.

It produced no change in the conduct of Paul. He continued to associate with the Gentiles freely, but for his own person at least when among the Jews, because he wished to preach to them, he still kept the law. But it by no means followed that he regarded it as necessary. On the contrary, he continually taught that it was a matter of entire indifference. There is no trace in his letters that he ever had anything to say about the use of blood, but he often spoke against fornication. In 1 Corinthians he told them that of itself the use of meats offered to idols was perfectly proper; but for the sake of the conscience of the weaker brethren who would thereby be offended, they ought to abstain from its use. This was therefore wholly in accordance with the agreement made in the council. It cannot be said that it affected Paul in any way in his mission work.[1] He con-

[1] It is perfectly clear that Paul denied any *religious* value to the observance of the law. It would logically follow that as a *religious* obligation it was no longer binding on the Jew any more than on the Gentile. So far Paul went. But did it follow that the Jew ought to cease to observe the law? Not at all, for that would be to give up his nationality. Paul seems not to have taught the Jews to cease observing the law, but only to have put such observance on the proper basis; that is, the Jew might continue to observe the law as a *national*, not as a religious duty. Among the Jews Paul seems to have lived as a Jew, but among the Gentiles he certainly *to some extent, if not wholly*, disregarded the law. He adopted the policy of being all things to all men, a Jew to the Jews, a Gentile to the Gentiles (1 Cor. ix. 18–23). What can that mean except that among the Gentiles he lived as the Gentiles? Again, at Antioch (Gal. ii. 11–21) Paul implies that both he and Peter, although Jews, had ceased to live as Jews, and were living as Gentiles. And yet the Acts say that Paul thought the Jews ought to keep the law and saw that he himself kept it. For Timothy was a Jew, and so had to be circumcised. If the account in Acts xxi. 17–26 is true, Paul took upon himself the vow of the four men for the express purpose of proving to the Jews and the Jewish Christians of Jerusalem that he had *not* been teaching the Jews to forsake Moses, to cease cir-

tinued to preach among the Jews wherever he went, and although he may not have urged them to give up the observance of the law, he certainly taught that it was of no religious value, but that they were to be made members of the Messiah's kingdom by believing in him, and not by their works of the law. In this he may have acted in accordance with the letter of the agreement, but hardly in the spirit of it. As is so often the case in agreements that partake of the nature of a compromise, each party regarded the result as a victory for itself, and acted accordingly. It was certainly very quickly disregarded by all, and neither the Judaizers nor Paul regarded themselves as bound by it. The only result of the council therefore was that the Gentiles were recognized as Christians by James, Peter, and John, but the line of separation between them and the Jewish Christians was more closely drawn than ever. The question had still to be decided. The real struggle was yet to come. The Council had but cleared the deck for action. It had made plain to all parties what the real issue was. And this was fought out between Paul and the Judaizers in the next years, which were so full of trial and bitterness of spirit for Paul.

cumcising their children and to desert the customs, and that *he himself also walked orderly, keeping the law.* Others may decide whether this is contradictory to Paul's principle as expressed in his authentic letters.

CHAPTER VII.

THE BEST YEARS OF PAUL.[1]

From the Council to Paul's arrest in the spring of 58 is a period of about eight years, which include his best work, his widest travels, his greatest influence, and his most successful labors. Above all, to this period belong his most important letters, which have been justly regarded as the most precious heirlooms of this great man. Thanks to the account in the Acts, which becomes more exact and detailed, and especially to the letters which he wrote, we are able to follow him more closely and to construct a much more complete history of him during this period than at any other time of his life. Compared with this period, all his previous labors had been very circumscribed. But now his horizon extends itself. He begins to look beyond Asia into Europe. At first he thought he would be satisfied if he could see Rome, but it soon became known to him that Rome already had a large and flourishing congregation, and as it was his principle not to linger where others had labored and planted Christianity, his thoughts ran on to Spain,

---

[1] Read Acts xv. 36–xxi. 26. 1 and 2 Thessalonians, Galatians, 1 and 2 Corinthians, and Romans.

and it became his fixed purpose to carry the Gospel to that far-off land.

We also notice a change in his policy from this time. He had traveled with only one or two helpers before this, but he now begins to surround himself with his young disciples, to train them for the work and to send them out to carry on his mission work, sometimes in new fields, sometimes in places where he had already established a congregation. In this way he multiplied himself and greatly increased his influence. But there was another change which was quite as important. He had indeed for a few years been in Antioch and had made that the centre of his labors. But when he set out on his journey with Barnabas, he seems not to have confined himself to the large cities, but even in the villages by the way he had stopped to preach. But during this period he changed his policy and began to lay much more emphasis on the work in the cities. He seems to have felt that it would be impossible for him to evangelize the whole world, but with the instinct of a genuine conqueror he determined to plant Christianity in the great centres of life and trade. And so we find him spending eighteen months at Corinth and soon afterward beginning a three years' residence in Ephesus. These eight years are generally divided into two periods of nearly equal length, and called respectively the second and third missionary journeys. For the sake of convenience these designations may be retained, but it must be remembered that nearly half of the time occupied by the first missionary journey was spent at Corinth, and almost all the third one was spent at Ephesus. From this it will be seen that they were not so much journeys as a change of residence.

Some time after the council at Jerusalem it is said that Paul proposed to Barnabas to revisit the churches which they had established. According to the language of the Acts it might be inferred that Paul's purpose was simply to revisit these, and that he had no thought of extending his work. But Paul undoubtedly, as we know from other sources, had a desire to penetrate further into Asia Minor, and as he must pass by his congregations he wished to revisit them by the way. Barnabas wished to take Mark with them again, but Paul was by no means willing to trust him a second time. He had deserted them and refused to go with them to the work once, and Paul was unwilling to give him another trial. There was a sharp contention between them, of a purely personal nature, and as they could not agree they separated, each going his own way. Barnabas took Mark and sailed away to Cyprus and is lost to our view, for we have no more information about him except the single reference in 1 Cor. ix. 5, from which we infer that he was still at work in the year 56. But we know nothing more about him. It is possible that he wrote the letter to the "Hebrews," for this is almost certainly not by Paul, although it has been attributed to him. But this is only a supposition; there is no direct proof that Barnabas wrote it.

But Paul chose Silas, who had been until recently a resident of Jerusalem, and began his journey into the interior of Asia Minor. It is barely possible that this Silas is identical with the Silvanus who is named in 1 Peter v. 12, since Silvanus was often contracted into Silas. This would be another connecting link between Peter and Paul.

They chose the land route, and from Antioch passed through Syria into Cilicia and then up into Cappadocia to Derbe and Lystra. Only the barest outlines of the journey are given. They revisited the churches there and encouraged and strengthened them. It was probably at Lystra that Paul found "a certain disciple named Timothy, the son of a believing Jewess, but his father was a Greek." He was already favorably known as a Christian missionary, and enjoyed the confidence and good opinion of the brethren in those parts. Recognizing his ability, Paul was determined that he should go with him to a wider field of labor and usefulness. Since his mother was a Jewess, Timothy was also regarded as a Jew. In accordance with his principle of being a Jew to the Jews, and a Greek to the Greeks, he now had Timothy circumcised, that he might have a ready entrance into the society of the Jews wherever he came. Though free from the law, for the sake of others he could sacrifice his freedom, that he might thereby bring them into a greater freedom. Though not bound to regard the prejudices and ignorance of others, the law of Christ, which is the law of love and service, made him the servant of all. So long as his fundamental principle was not in question, he could, on the principle of Christian brotherly love, yield everything. Besides, Timothy was regarded as a Jew, and the common opinion was that the law was still binding on the Jews.

From this region, Paul and his companions turned to the west into Phrygia, and it is probable that even at this time Paul had it in mind to go to Ephesus. That is evidently the inference to be drawn from the expression in Acts xvi. 6, " Having been forbidden to speak the word in Asia." " Asia" was the name of the Roman province which was formed by the three ancient divisions, Lydia, Caria, and Lycia, the capital of which was Ephesus. They wished to pass from Phrygia into this province, but something which was interpreted as the disapproval of the Holy Spirit prevented them, so they turned back from Phrygia into Galatia. Here as we have seen, Paul was taken sick (Gal. iv. 13). He was no longer able to travel, but he could still preach the gospel, so his illness resulted in the establishment of Christianity among the Galatians. We have no details of the work done in this region, since the author of the Acts simply says that " they went through the region of Phrygia and Galatia." In Gal. iv. 13 Paul only refers to his illness, which was of such a character as to render him an object of loathing and disgust to the Gentiles, but they had received him as an angel, nay, even as Christ himself; a remarkable expression, showing how eagerly the gospel was accepted by many of the Gentiles, because it so completely satisfied the deepest longings of their heart.

Passing through Galatia they intended to go into Bithynia, but again something intervened which closed the way to them. They were now hemmed in. The way to the southeast they had just traveled; the ways to the southwest and to the north were closed to them. There were but two possibilities left. They could turn to the northeast into Paphlagonia, or to the western coast, from which the passage to Europe was easy. There is an uneasiness and restlessness in his motions that show that Paul's horizon was widening. The thought of establishing his gospel in Europe had taken hold of his mind. Paul seems to have felt the greatness of the occasion. Apparently not stopping to preach anywhere, he hastened through Mysia to Troas, for already he felt the premonitions of the call to a more distant field. He would have been glad to remain in Asia, for he saw much to do there. But he was impelled forward, though still full of uncertainty as to whether he should go to Europe or not.

It was a period of most painful uncertainty and doubt for him, which has left its traces in his letters to the Corinthians. He was conscious of the great national differences between the Greeks of the mainland of Europe and the mixed peoples of Asia. The Greeks loved the beautiful to such an extent that they were really unable to appreciate anything unless it were presented in a pleasing form. A technical knowledge and application of rhetoric and the use of fine language were among the first requisites in a public speaker among them. Paul knew that he was not a trained rhetorician, nor a philosopher acquainted with all the systematic teachings and formulas of the schools of thought and able to present his gospel in such a way as to make it attractive to the æsthetic and philosophical Greeks. The Greeks were accustomed to being entertained and pleased by traveling rhetoricians and philosophers. Was it possible that he would be able to compete against these with his simple gospel of the death and resurrection of Christ? We know that he had a peculiar style of rhetoric and dialectics, though they were not those of the schools, but he modestly estimated this very low. From his own words, we may be sure that he never felt at home on this Greek soil. In Athens, as we shall see, he made little impression, and at Corinth he was unable to hide the fact that he felt this weakness and was filled with fear and trembling for the result. And this very weakness of the apostle was afterwards used as the ground of contempt by some of his opponents, in their attempt to alienate the affections of the Corinthians from him. All these considerations now made him hesitate. But in this state of doubt and indecision the "vision of the man of Macedonia" determined his course. He regarded the dream as an indication that it was the will of God that he should go and preach the gospel unto them also.

And here begin those remarkable "we" pieces which continue with some interruptions to the end of the book. These exhibit their true character at once. They are undoubtedly from the diary of an eye-witness. He indicates that they had a favorable wind, for they made a straight course to Samothrace, a large island in the Ægean Sea, and this lasted but one day, "for on the day following" they reached Neapolis. By selecting the passages in which "we" occurs, and noting these little peculiarities, we get a good idea of this diary, which served as one of the sources for the history we have in the Acts. But unfortunately the author never tells us his name, or how he came into the society of Paul, or why he accompanied him. He never once indulges in personal reminiscences, or autobiographical details. His modesty is commendable, but we are the losers by it. How interesting it would be if he had but given us the pages on which he described his first interview with Paul, or the first sermon he heard from his lips, or the impression which the first message of the gospel made upon him.

Neapolis was but the port of Philippi, which was eight miles distant from the coast. Here we see one of the first traces of Paul's change of policy in regard to the cities. He passed by Neapolis and went at once to the great city of Philippi. This was near a famous battle ground, for it was on the plains of Philippi that in the year 42 B. C. the civil war that followed the murder of Julius Cæsar was ended. Here Octavius and Antony met and overcame Brutus and Cassius, who in despair ended their lives.[1] In honor of this victory, which opened the way for all his future greatness, Octavius made Philippi a Roman colony. That is, the inhabitants were made Roman citizens and the city received the laws and government of Rome.

In Philippi there were not many Jews. They seem not even to have had a synagogue, but only "a place of prayer." Outside the city walls, under the shadow of the trees on the river bank, they found a few women who had come together, and they sat down among them and told them the story of the cross. Of these women some were Jewish proselytes; another fact in proof of what has been already said in regard to the missionary efforts of the Jews. Although there were so few Jews in Philippi that they did not have a house for their meetings, yet they had made proselytes, and that too among the better classes. One of these was Lydia, who had come from Thyatira and settled in Philippi that she might carry on the sale of the finely colored garments which were exported from her home in the province of Lydia. If not a proselyte, she was at least "one that feared God." She was apparently rich, for she had a house and was able to entertain Paul and his company of helpers, which now numbered at least four persons.

They remained in Philippi probably some

[1] In connection with Philippi see Shakespeare, *Julius Cæsar*, Act V.

months, during which time they seem not to have had any other place of worship than the place of prayer already mentioned. There is no trace of any struggle with the Jews, who, we are led to infer, were persuaded by Paul and believed in Christ. Their stay here was abruptly ended by a persecution the cause of which is minutely described. We meet here again with one of those strange cases so frequently mentioned in ancient writers, which baffle us because we have no scientific description of them, and all the information that we have about them is so colored by the superstitions of the age that it is impossible to form a clear idea of the nature of the disease. It is probable that this "maid having a spirit of divination" was suffering from hysteria or some similar form of nervous and mental disease, and that her masters had control over her to such an extent that they could in some way force her to fall into a fit of hysteria. In this condition she spoke with a strange tone, which the ancients called ventriloquism, and was regarded as the peculiar speech of soothsayers and fortune-tellers. It was the common belief that the poor creatures thus afflicted could foretell the future, and her masters were thus imposing on the credulity of the people and using her for the purpose of making gain, a very common form of swindle practiced in those days. "But when her masters saw that the hope of their gain was gone, they laid hold on Paul and Silas and dragged them into the market place before the rulers." But they were careful to frame their charges in such a way as to make it appear that Paul and Silas were offending against the laws of the state. In the first place, it was said that they were Jews. Of course this in itself was not a criminal offense; it was only an appeal to the popular dislike of the Jews. Being Jews, it was to be expected that they had done something offensive and worthy of punishment. The real charge was that they were trying to introduce a foreign religion, one that was regarded as unlawful. Attention has already been called to the fact that Eastern religions were forbidden in the West, and Paul and Silas were charged with having acted contrary to this law. "These men, being Jews, do exceedingly trouble our city, and set forth customs which it is not lawful for us to receive, or to observe, being Romans" (Acts xvi. 20, 21). The trial is passed over so rapidly that we cannot follow it. It appears that the crowd made a demonstration against them, and that the magistrates, probably without an examination, ordered them to be beaten with rods and then put into prison.

On the following day the magistrates sent their officers to have them released, but now Paul declares that they are Roman citizens and that the magistrates must make certain amends for having beaten them. Beating with rods was a punishment for slaves, but free Roman citizens were protected against all such dishonoring forms of punishment. But why did Paul allow himself to be beaten? Why did he not at once declare that he was a Roman citizen? What purpose can he have had in allowing himself thus to be beaten when he might by a word have escaped it? Questions which we cannot answer. Perhaps he submitted to the punishment in order that he might get some power over the magistrates by being able to assume the position of an injured party. Perhaps he thought he could thereby make better terms with them, and so secure the Christians from all molestation. It is possible too that the magistrates paid no attention to his claims to Roman citizenship, for Paul himself says that he had been three times beaten with rods (2 Cor. xi. 25). This was the Roman form of punishment, while the Jews used scourges. So that three times at least his Roman citizenship had not protected him. Paul also refers to this in his first letter to the Thessalonians (ii. 2), where he reminds them that in spite of his sufferings and the shameful treatment which he had received at Philippi, he had boldly preached the gospel of God to them.

The church at Philippi is especially interesting to us on many accounts. There were few Jews there, and this seems to have had some effect on its history and development. It remained true to Paul, and we have no traces of the work and influence of the Judaizers among its members. The letter which Paul wrote to this church from Rome, about the year 62, is one of the most interesting and charming that we have from his pen.

From the whole tone of the letter, as well as from the many endearing expressions which occur in it, we might justly say that it was Paul's favorite congregation. From this letter, as well as from the Acts, we learn that there was a unique, intimate relation existing between them. No other congregation seems to have come so close to Paul's heart. This is apparent from two facts; the one, that Paul allowed himself to be entertained by one of its members, the other that on several occasions he accepted money from them. It was entirely contrary to his custom to be entertained by his converts, for he generally worked with his hands and supported himself by his own labors, that he might not seem to be making gain out of the gospel. But at Philippi, from some cause or other, he saw that he could allow himself to be entertained by Lydia without incurring such a charge. And several times afterward they sent him money to relieve his wants. While he was at Thessalonica they sent him money " once and again," or as we would say, " a few times " (Phil. iv. 16). While he was at Corinth he refused to receive any support in any way from the Corinthians, although he was in want. Yet Silas and Timothy, when they came from Macedonia, brought him further gifts from the churches there. But this was not a passing affection for the apostle on the part of the Philippians. It lasted throughout his whole life. For, years afterward, when he was a prisoner in Rome, they again sent him money by the hand of Epaphroditus, one of their number. We know little of the history of the congregation, but it seems to have been noted for its liberality. From 2 Cor. viii. 1–5, we learn that its members were subjected to a good deal of persecution, but that in spite of this they were contributing largely to the funds that were being collected for the poor at Jerusalem.

His stay in Philippi was cut short by the scourging and imprisonment. The magistrates, fearing the violence of the mob, asked them to leave the city. They were not ordered to go away, but as Paul always had regard for the public peace and never wantonly provoked opposition of any kind, they called the brethren together, comforted them, and took their departure.

Their next field of labor was Thessalonica, a large city having a numerous Jewish population. At this time there was a severe famine in the city and the neighboring country, and there was much want and distress there. This accounts therefore for the fact that the Philippians sent him money during his stay in Thessalonica (Phil. iv. 16). As usual, Paul began in the synagogue, proving from the Scriptures of the Old Testament that the common Messianic expectations were false, but that the Messiah should suffer, and then showing how these prophecies had been fulfilled in the history of Jesus. The make-up of this congregation is clearly stated. *Some* of the Jews were persuaded, but evidently not many of them. A great multitude of the Greeks that had already been under the influence of the teachings of Judaism, and quite a number of women who were members of the principal families in the city, believed. Here, as everywhere else, women of rank and wealth had embraced the principal truths of Judaism, but now readily accepted Christianity and were of the greatest influence in spreading it among the members of their households.

But the Jews were stirred up by the success of Paul in spreading what they regarded as abominable heresy, and began an agitation against him which was destined to make Thessalonica unsafe for him and so to compel him to leave. Since they were Jews their opposition must have been purely from religious motives, but, as is generally the case, the means employed were far from being religious. They easily found the means of gathering a mob of the lazy loafers that throng the streets of every southern city, ready for any act of violence that offers either pleasure or profit. With these they assaulted the house of Jason, who was apparently one of the principal converts, and dragged him and some of the other brethren before the magistrates. They very shrewdly kept their religious hatred in the background, and preferred only political charges against them. It is interesting to note how easily the language of the gospel could be made to appear treasonable. Paul certainly preached that Jesus was the Messiah, that he had established the kingdom of God, but the

Jews clearly knew that he did not preach that Jesus was to be made king in the place of the Roman emperor. There was nothing in his preaching that would lead to a revolt against the Roman government. Yet his language could easily be so twisted and garbled as to make it appear that he was preaching treason and endeavoring to set up another kingdom.

They gave the Messiahship of Jesus a political coloring, for they knew that no other charge would so quickly arouse the government to vigorous action as the danger of a political insurrection. The character of the Jew is apparent in this whole transaction. Everywhere he was turbulent, and always causing the Roman authorities trouble; at every opportunity he stirred up a mob and raised the standard of revolt. He was the most unpatriotic, the least Roman, of all the nationalities that formed a part of the Empire. But now, when it served his purpose, he could throw up his hat and shout for Cæsar, and be the first to denounce the followers of "another king, Jesus." In this attempt against Paul they were unsuccessful, for they were unable to find him. Jason and his friends were able to give security that he would keep the peace, and to persuade the authorities that he was not guilty of treason, so he was set free. But the city was no longer safe for Paul and Silas. They were sent away to Berœa by night. From this fact we may form some estimate of the danger of the situation. But although Paul and Silas escaped, the Christians whom they left behind were exposed to many persecutions. In the course of a few months at most, Paul reached Corinth, from which place he wrote the two letters to the Thessalonians. By studying these we are able to glean some information about the condition of the church and the character and contents of the gospel which he preached.

In the first letter he praises them very much, that they had accepted the gospel in the face of opposition and persecution. They had become imitators of Christ and of Paul in that they had "received the word in much affliction." They had also become imitators of the Christian churches in Judæa, for as the Jewish Christians had suffered at the hands of the unbelieving Jews, so also the heathen Christians at Thessalonica had suffered at the hands of their heathen neighbors. In the second chapter Paul indulges in a kind of review of his conduct while he was among them, reminding them of the kind of life he had led while there, his manner of dealing with each one, his blameless conduct, and his many exhortations that they "should walk worthily of God," who was calling them into his glorious kingdom.

We learn, too, that Paul had been compelled to leave Thessalonica before he was sure that the gospel had been firmly established, and he had earnestly desired to return to them. Indeed he seems to have made an effort more than once to get back, but "Satan" hindered him, which means that because of the persecutions and opposition he had not been able to return. But since he himself could not come, he had sent Timothy to comfort and strengthen them and to encourage them in the persecution that was troubling them so. Timothy had just returned to him at Corinth, bringing good news from them, which comforted him, although he himself was in great distress and affliction. Something was oppressing him, and he seems to have been unable to work with all his accustomed energy in Corinth, until Timothy and Silas joined him. The good news which they brought from the churches in Macedonia, and especially from the Thessalonians, at once cheered him, and he "was constrained by the word," as the author of the Acts expresses it (xviii. 5). Paul regarded it as a new lease of life, for he wrote them, "For now we live, if ye stand fast in the Lord."

But he still hoped to return to them, for night and day he was praying that he might see their face again, and that God would direct his way to them. But it was some years before Paul actually was able to go to Thessalonica again, and we know nothing at all of the condition in which he found them then. The fourth chapter begins with a discussion of two closely related questions which had to be discussed in every church that was established among the Gentiles, namely, those of chastity and of marriage. The prevailing heathen ideas and practices were so far from what they should have been, that especial efforts had to be made to secure the proper conduct on the part of the heathen Christians. The question of the resurrection and the fate of those who died before the coming of Christ were also troubling the Thessalonians, and Paul takes this opportunity of assuring them that it is immaterial whether they live until Christ comes or not. For those who have died will be raised from the dead, and those that are still alive will be caught up in the air to meet the Lord, and, what was of most importance, they should all " be forever with the Lord." But for his appearance all should be continually on the watch, for no one knows the time of his coming. And this watchfulness consists in the proper kind of life, in living as is becoming the sons of light. They should be sober, and guard and fight against sin of every kind. Some of their number had taken it upon themselves to labor for the spread of the gospel, and for their edification and instruction. Since all such had voluntarily taken upon themselves this work of love, they were to be highly esteemed and regarded with honor for the work's sake. The disorderly should be admonished, the fearful ones encouraged, the weak supported. Above all the spirit must not be quenched, but each one should have the right to speak whatever message he might have received. These prophesyings should not be despised, but they were to be tested, and that which is good and approved must be held fast.

The second letter [1] was written very soon afterwards. The first letter had undoubtedly had good effect on them, but there were some questions still agitating them, and there were signs of an increasingly unhealthy condition. The persecutions and troubles from the heathen were still continued. Perhaps that had something to do with the growing enthusiasm that was now threatening to injure the congregation. They were all especially interested in the question of the return of Christ, and many of them had given up their occupations, had quit their work, and were spending their time in discussing this. It had already led to great disorder in the congregation. Paul rebukes all such, and emphasized the fact that all Christians should attend to their duties, living soberly, quietly, and honorably before all.

In regard to the second coming of Christ, Paul probably made the matter very clear to the Thessalonians in the first twelve verses of the second chapter. They may have understood it, but it is certain that no one now knows what he meant. His language is simply inexplicable. Every one who has written about it has had some more or less ingenious explanation of it, but no one is able to say what it means. It is hopelessly dark and obscure. He speaks of the " falling away," but of the

---

[1] There are many who question the genuineness of the second letter to the Thessalonians. There are some difficulties connected with it, but it is by no means sure that this is not a genuine letter of the Apostle Paul.

falling away of what? And of "the man of sin, the son of perdition," who exalts himself against all that is called God, or that is worshiped; he sits in the temple of God, he claims to be God, but who or what this is, it is impossible to say. There is something that restrains, but what it is, or what it restrains, is not clear. "The mystery of lawlessness is already at work," he says, but what this is still remains a mystery. Something restrains until something is taken out of the way, but there is no clew as to what either of the "somethings" is. And then the "lawless one shall be revealed," but who he is, no one knows. The language is all so indefinite that it can easily be made to apply to almost anything, and so the commentators have all tried to exhibit their originality and penetration of intellect by giving out some new and startling interpretation of this passage. It is safe to say that no one has been able to solve its difficulties. It is curious to note that some one had already been forging letters in Paul's name (ii. 2), and he saw himself compelled to guard against all such forgeries in the future by signing his letters himself (iii. 17).

From Thessalonica they came to Berœa, where they had more success among the Jews than in any other place. Apparently the majority of the Jews there believed, as well as many of their proselytes. But the Jews of Thessalonica are said to have followed them to Berœa, and to avoid the danger Paul was sent off to Athens, but Silas and Timothy remained in Macedonia.

Paul waited in Athens for the coming of Silas and Timothy. Whether they actually came, or not, we cannot tell. It is probable that Timothy came alone, but Paul was so exercised in mind about the Thessalonians that he at once sent him back to Macedonia to visit and strengthen them (1 Thess. iii. 2.) But although alone in Athens, he was by no means idle. He was in the very citadel of heathenism, of idolatry. Athens was the seat of the greatest university in the world, and its professors were of course all heathen. It exerted the greatest influence on the thought and culture of the world. It long remained *the* university, and even Christian parents sent their children there to be educated. Some of the great church fathers received their education at the heathen university of Athens. It became the centre of literary and philosophical opposition to Christianity until 529 A. D., when the Emperor Justinian drove out the professors and forbade all further instruction to be given by heathen teachers. At this time it was the home of philosophy and philosophers. They wandered about through the streets, market-places, and cool colonnades, surrounded by their pupils, discussing the highest and most important questions as well as the most trivial.

But Athens was also the home of the gods, for no other city had so many fine temples as she. Only a few of them are still standing, and although desolate and robbed of their ornaments and works of art, they are still the wonder and admiration of the world. She was rich in works of art of all kinds, but especially in statues. They were everywhere. The temples, the market-places, and even the streets were crowded with them, so that one writer said that in Athens it was easier to find a god than a man. But Athens was now falling into decay. Her supremacy had passed away. Her sister city, Corinth, had robbed her of her commerce, and she was no longer the capital, but ranked as a provincial city. Her visitors were composed largely of students and philosophers, artists, and pilgrims, who came to study or worship at her famous altars. The great tide of travel between the East and the West swept past without touching her. She was now neglected, and nearly a hundred years were to pass away before the world should again be filled with admiration and veneration for her. She was yet to experience a period of restoration and renovation, and even of wealth and prosperity, but at this time her fortunes and name were at their ebb. Time and the rest of the world had sped on, leaving her by the way. And as in some sleepy, inland college town, where the pulse-beats of life are slow and the sharp competition and stir of commerce are unknown, the people spent their time in the discussion of the most varied topics. All the life she had was intellectual, all her energies were consumed in discussion.

The genius of Paul is again made apparent by his conduct here. He easily adapted himself to the situation, and adopted the methods of the philosophers, and went about through the streets entering into conversation whenever opportunity presented itself. He met some of the philosophers themselves, and to the gaping crowds that gathered about him he told the story of the cross and of the resurrection. But they did not understand him. It seemed to them that he was trying to introduce two new gods, whom he called Jesus and the Resurrection. They were greatly interested in that, for what could be more interesting to them than the announcement of a new god? And here were two of them at once! It seems strange to us that they should have thought of the Resurrection as a god, but we must remember that they had peopled the groves with gods; they looked upon every stream as the home of spirits, and the winds as manifestations of various gods. In short they brought everything into direct connection with some god; hence it is not strange that they thought of Jesus and of the Resurrection as new gods, with whose powers they were eager to become acquainted. The crowd of curious listeners was so great that a larger space was necessary, and in their eagerness they hurried him up to the broad rocky plateau overlooking the city, and asked him to explain his teaching at greater length. And here on Mars' Hill, in the midst of the expectant throng, Paul preached one of the greatest sermons of his life. It was a supreme moment in his life and in the history of Christianity. The simple gospel which had its beginning in the far-off Galilee was here face to face with the representatives and teachers of the world's religion. It was like "bearding the lion in his den," for Christianity was here attacking the very stronghold of polytheism. There is something dramatic in the situation and impressive in the thought. The occasion was inspiring, and Paul felt the importance of the hour. The author of the Acts felt it, too, for in describing this his style and language became more elevated.

Paul's text was "The unknown God." It is a fact attested by more than one reliable ancient author that there were altars in Athens erected to unknown divinities, and as Paul had been wandering about through the city, his eye caught one of those strange inscriptions which furnished him with both text and sermon. The thought of this address is akin to that of the first three chapters of Romans, where Paul declares that God had written his law in the hearts of the heathen. For Paul sees in the Athenians a deep religious sense, perverted to idols, to be sure, and mixed with much ignorance and superstition, but still in its inmost purpose inspired by, and directed to, the one true God. In the fact that they had erected altars to an unknown god, Paul sees the proof that their many gods had not satisfied them; there were aspirations and desires which their known gods did not fulfil. The deeper thoughts and affections of the soul looked beyond the known gods to one although unknown, yet dimly felt, who would satisfy the soul thus feeling after its Creator.

So Paul begins, not with a tirade on the sin of idolatry, but, genius-like, finding common ground on which to stand with them, and naturally and beautifully introducing his message of the one true God. He did all he could to put his audience and himself on good terms with each other, for he began his address with a compliment to his hearers. The Athenians were proud of the reputation which they enjoyed of being devotedly religious. Every god found a welcome among them, and a temple or an altar where he might be worshiped. Because of their care of the gods they were everywhere spoken of as the most religious people of the world. And Paul in his first sentence admitted that they indeed deserved this praise. "Ye men of Athens, I see that you are indeed very religious, for fearful lest through ignorance you should fail to pay the proper homage to all, you have even erected an altar with the inscription 'To an unknown God.'"[1] In a masterly way he assumes that this unknown God is the God of the Old Testament, the God whom Jesus had revealed as the

---

[1] King James's version as well as the Revisers by their false translation have here made Paul appear to be guilty of insulting the Athenians by his first words by declaring that they were very superstitious. But any one who reads the whole passage and considers its tone will see at once that Paul did not mean to insult them, but that he really recognized that their reputation was well founded, and that they were exceedingly religious, and to the best of their knowledge careful for the honor of the gods.

Father of all, and declares that he brings them a message from Him. He then sets forth his character. He is the Creator of all things, the Lord of Heaven and Earth; He needs nothing from his creatures, nay, rather, He gave them all they have. He it is that has created all men of one race, and hence all are his offspring, his children. He does not dwell in temples made by our hands, for He is exalted above all such things. Since we are his children, we ought to suppose that we resemble Him, and from what we know of ourselves we ought to be able to form a better estimate of Him and of his character. We ought not to think that He can be worthily represented by any statue, of whatever material. From our own character, our sense of right and wrong, of justice, and from all the nobler qualities which we possess, we ought to be able to think of Him in a far more becoming way. Paul appeals to their moral sense. This unknown God now calls on men everywhere to repent, for He has appointed a day of judgment on which all will receive rewards or punishments according to their conduct. He has given a sure proof of this in that He raised up the man Jesus from the dead.

The resurrection of the dead was a stumbling-block to the Greeks, and at the mention of this some mocked; others said, "We will hear you again," a polite way of saying that they were not persuaded by his words. He had little success there. The gospel was too simple for them. It may be remarked here that Christianity was generally not acceptable to the Greeks until the simple teaching of Christ, the most of which deals with character and conduct, was perverted into a philosophical, speculative, theological system, and the essence of religion was made to consist in knowledge instead of the childlike attitude of the heart toward God.

But what impression did all the beauties of Athens make on Paul? Probably he was insensible to her æsthetic side, the beauty of her temples, and her works of art. For Paul was a Jew, and the Jews were bitterly opposed to all representations of the human body. And besides, much of the art was idolatrous, and hence must have been an abomination in his eyes. But his greatness was apparent in the fact that he did not indulge in invective or violence, but in their idolatry sought for some great thought that would lead them to the recognition of a higher truth.

Corinth formed, in almost every respect, a sharp contrast to Athens. It was a port lying on the highway between the East and West, the resort of sailors, who have always been noted the world over for their bad morals. It was one of the great markets of the world, and hence the resort of merchants from every part of the Empire. It has always been observed that the majority of travelers leave their character at home, and lead while among strangers a free and easy life. Corinth abounded in temptations of every kind. Gambling was carried on to a frightful extent, and the very name of Corinth had become a by-word because of the evil reputation of her women. There was here a famous temple of Aphrodite, a part of whose worship consisted in breaking the seventh commandment. And here were hundreds of women who passed their lives in the temple or visited it regularly in the service of this goddess. It was probably the most immoral city in the world.

Here Paul made the acquaintance of two persons who were to be of the greatest service and comfort to him. Aquila and Priscilla had recently come from Rome, in consequence of the action of the Emperor Claudius, who forbade the Jews to hold their meetings in Rome. They were tent-makers, too, and by means of their common occupation he was able to make their acquaintance and enter into close relations with them. We are not told whether they were already Christians, or not; at any rate they were soon his best helpers. It is curious to note that at first the name of Aquila precedes that of his wife, but soon her name takes the first place, from which it has been inferred that she was probably the abler of the two, and more efficient in the work. They remained with Paul throughout his whole stay of eighteen months in Corinth, went with him to Ephesus, where they took a house and made it the centre for missionary operations, making it the place of meeting for all the Christians near them, thus establishing a "church in their house." They were still in

Ephesus when Paul wrote the first letter to the Corinthians, and he could write to their former friends and acquaintance in Corinth, " Aquila and Priscilla send you their very best greetings." A year or two later, when he wrote the letter to the Romans, they had returned to their former home in Rome, had again taken a house, and were pursuing the same course as in Ephesus.

In Corinth, as has been said, Paul was rejoined by Timothy and Silas, who came from Macedonia bringing good news, which so cheered Paul that he began to prosecute his work with greater energy and enthusiasm. From here he wrote the two letters to the Thessalonians, which have already been discussed.

As usually happened, only some of the Jews believed, and the opposition became so great that he was compelled to quit visiting the synagogue and to open another place of worship and meeting for the Christians. For this purpose he secured the house of Titus Justus, who either was a proselyte, or had been under Jewish instruction. For it is said that he was "one who worshiped God." Of all these eighteen months there is recorded only one event, which shows how very sketchy and incomplete the book of Acts is as history. Toward the end of the reign of Claudius, Gallio was made proconsul of the province of Achaia, which includes all Greece. This must have been in the year 53 or 54. Gallio was the brother of the famous stoic philosopher and writer, Seneca, both of whom were put to death by Nero. He was himself the author of several plays and works on science. He was a learned man, the friend and companion of many of the greatest literary men of his day. He was noted, too, for his mild and gentle disposition. Seneca, his brother, showed his love for him by dedicating some of his works to him.[1]

The Jews are again represented as the cause of the trouble and opposition. They brought Paul before Gallio with the charge that he was teaching men to worship God contrary to their law. They did not attempt to hide the real nature of the charges and there was no resort to any political accusations. It seems strange that they should have made purely religious charges against any one before the local magistrates, for in religious matters the Jewish synagogues are supposed everywhere to have had independent jurisdiction. Gallio looked upon the whole matter as one of little moment. He was angry that they should have disturbed him and tried to make him the judge in the matter of their

[1] This contact of Paul with Gallio was probably in part the basis of the famous forgery of the correspondence of Paul and Seneca. But only in part, for the Christians of the third and fourth centuries, like some of a much later day, could not admit that the heathen were capable of producing anything good. But in the writings of Seneca they found much that agreed with the best Christian principles. The only way to solve the problem was to declare that Seneca had known Paul and had got all his good things from him. To support this, these letters were forged, in which Paul is made to impart the Christian teachings to Seneca. The letters were for a long time regarded as genuine, but they are undoubtedly a forgery, and cannot be earlier than the third century.

law. It was only a Jewish theological quarrel and they might settle it among themselves. He was willing to act as judge in matters which involved the principle of right and wrong, but in their wars about words he would take no part. With this rebuke he ordered them to be driven from his presence. But this was not the end of the matter. They had dug a pit for another, they themselves were yet to fall into it. Their turbulence and troublesomeness had made even the mild Gallio impatient and indifferent, and the fickle mob took advantage of the opportunity to vent their dislike upon them. They laid hold of Sosthenes, who had been made ruler of the synagogue in place of Crispus who had become a Christian, and gave him a sound beating. It seems to have had a good effect on him, for later we find that he had become a Christian and was in Ephesus with Paul when he wrote the first letter to the Corinthians.

For a year and a half Paul remained in Corinth. Whether he was in the city all the time or not it is impossible to say. But Christianity certainly spread beyond the limits of the city, for the second letter is addressed not only to the " church of God which is at Corinth," but also to " all the saints which are in the whole of Achaia." At length the time came for a change of residence. He evidently thought that Christianity was firmly established in Corinth, so he and Aquila and Priscilla sailed away to Asia, intending to establish themselves there. In regard to the vow which is spoken of, only two things are clear; first, that there was a vow, and second, that it was fulfilled at Corinth. But it is by no means clear who had made the vow, or what its purport was. From the Greek it is impossible to say to whom it refers. It may have been either Aquila or Paul, though one has the impression that the author had Paul in mind. It was not a Nazarite vow, but Paul, if it was he, had vowed that he would accomplish a certain thing, and as a sign of the vow until it was accomplished he would not allow his hair to be cut; for that was the ordinary form of such vows, which were by no means uncommon.

They landed at Ephesus, where Aquila and Priscilla remained, but Paul is said to have gone on to Cæsarea, and from there he "went up," that is, to Jerusalem, and after saluting the church there returned to Antioch. Here he remained only a short time and then set out through Asia Minor, passing through Galatia and Phrygia to Ephesus, where he had long desired to establish Christianity. This is the beginning of what is commonly called the third missionary journey, but it was rather simply a change of residence from Corinth to Ephesus, which now became his headquarters. Ephesus (since 133 B. C., when the Pergamenian kingdom passed into the hands of Rome) was the capital of the province of Asia, which consisted of Mysia, Lydia and Caria. Paul had an eye for the strategic points. Ephesus was a large and beautiful city, exceedingly rich, for her commerce was even greater than that of Corinth. She had almost all the advantages of a port town, although she was not directly on the sea. And she was the terminus of the great caravan route through Asia Minor to the East. Fine roads led to the interior of the country and gave excellent facilities for travel. She was in touch with both Europe and Asia, and from here Paul had a wide horizon, for he could be constantly in contact with people from all quarters of the Empire. Christianity was sure to spread along the lines of travel. Here was the seat of the worship of Artemis (or Diana, as it is improperly translated in both the authorized and revised versions) whose temple was one of the seven wonders of the world.

Paul certainly reached Ephesus in the year 54, but in the mean time a new apostle had appeared on the scene. Apollos had come from Alexandria to Ephesus. It is said that he was a learned man and mighty in the Scriptures, which means that he was trained in the allegorical method of interpretation and was very skillful in it. The church at Alexandria, which afterwards played such a prominent part in the history of the church and in the development of doctrine, is in the deepest obscurity until toward the end of the second century. This is one of the obscure notices from which we get all the knowledge we have of it, until suddenly at the end of the second century it springs into full view as the seat of a famous Christian catechetical school, with able teachers and a large and flourishing congregation. Now we learn that Apollos was engaged in preaching the gospel of Jesus. "He had been instructed in the way of the Lord," and he spoke and taught carefully and with great zeal the things concerning Jesus. That can only mean that he was a Christian, and that like Paul he was a traveling missionary. But the strange thing is that he knew nothing about a form of Christian baptism. He practiced baptism to be sure, but it was the baptism of John, that is, a baptism as the symbol of repentance and not in the name of Jesus. Here then we learn of two things that are both interesting and strange. The first is that the movement begun by John the Baptist had spread beyond the boundaries of Palestine. It had even reached Alexandria, where Apollos had learned of it and adopted it. The other is that there were Christians who did not practice baptism in the name of Jesus, but had an entirely different form. The same thing is to be observed in regard to the "certain disciples" spoken of in Acts xix. 1. They were Christians, but knew nothing of a form of Christian baptism. How such a state of affairs was possible it is difficult to say, but the fact cannot be questioned. How widely this type of Christianity without Christian baptism was spread, and how long it lasted, we cannot say, but the fact that it was in cities so widely separated as Alexandria and Ephesus, and that too nearly thirty years after the death of Christ, shows that there must have been many who either did not know of Christian baptism or did not regard it as essential, and that there must have been an extensive propagation of Christianity without a Christian form of baptism.

It is interesting to note that Christianity, although of this peculiar form, was thus early in Alexandria. Apollos was further instructed by Aquila and Priscilla, and, as he desired to pass over to Europe, took letters of introduction to the Christians at Corinth. It would seem that after Paul's departure from Corinth the Jews had been having the best of it in the many disputations which they had with the Christians. For intercourse was not wholly broken off between the Christians and the Jews, but they undoubtedly continued their discussions and arguments. But they were no match for Apollos, who was trained in the Alexandrian school of logic, philosophy, and exegesis, and knew the Scriptures thoroughly and was master of all the arts which are so necessary to the debater.

In Ephesus Paul again began with the Jews. Although there were Christians already there, yet they had not separated from the Jews, but were still attending the synagogue; they seem not to have had a separate place of worship. Paul continued this for three months, laboring to persuade the Jews of the Messiahship of Jesus, but at last the opposition was so great and violent that he had to withdraw from them. The school of Tyrannus was probably a building much like our "town halls," which was for rent and was used by the traveling philosophers, rhetoricians, teachers, and all such who wished to meet the public. Paul now rented this hall and made it the regular place of meeting for the Christians and the centre of his missionary work. Here for three years (xx. 31) he continued to teach and preach the gospel, extending his influence through his disciples and helpers until, as it is said, "All them that dwelt in Asia heard the word of the Lord, both Jews and Greeks." In these few years he laid the foundation of the future greatness of the church in Asia Minor. All the west part of the country must have been evangelized. There were many cities there, and undoubtedly the beginning of their churches falls in this period. In the next century Asia Minor is the stronghold of Christianity; the heathen temples were deserted, the animals of sacrifice remained unsold, and it seemed that all the people were turned Christian. That such progress was possible was due to the labors of Paul and his companions, with Ephesus for their headquarters.

The immediate success in Ephesus was very great. Many from all classes believed; even many of the religious mountebanks and swindlers were converted and gave up the practice of their deceptive arts. The Asiarchs, or as it is translated, "the chief officers of Asia" (xix. 31), were what we would call a standing committee that had charge of the temples, the sacrifices, the public games, and the great celebrations which frequently took place. They had to provide for all such events, make the necessary arrangements and preside over them, and so were in the very midst of the idolatrous life and practices of the people. And yet Paul had made friends, and we may certainly conclude disciples, among even these.

In these three years Christianity made great inroads on the heathenism of the city. So great were the numbers of its adherents, that toward the end of his stay here the trade in images of the goddess and her temple was so diminished that the workmen were losing their employment; there was so little demand for these objects. This led to a great demonstration on the part of the workmen against Paul. The account which we have of it is unfortunately very brief, but very lifelike. This Demetrius was a silversmith and the head of a firm which manufactured images of the goddess. We are accustomed to think of labor unions, and Knights of Labor, and all similar organizations as something quite modern, but they were just as frequent and prominent at that time in Asia Minor as to-day in America. The workmen of every particular craft formed a guild or labor union, and these numerous unions were united into a great organization. At the head of this was this Demetrius, who therefore occupied much the same position as the president of the Knights of Labor to-day. A great mass meeting of the " workmen of like occupation " was held, which was addressed by him. That is, it was a meeting of all those who were engaged in the manufacture of all those little statues which were so common in antiquity. They were made of gold, silver, bronze, and baser metals, often of clay, and the makers of all these are included under the " workmen of like occupation."

The excavations of Mr. Wood have brought to light a great many inscriptions and much material which throw light on this account in the Acts, and show that the author was well informed about various peculiar local customs which differed from those of other Greek cities. They show, too, what this chapter in the Acts also shows, that the temple and worship of Artemis, and the many interests connected therewith, dominated the life and thought of the whole city. In the inscriptions Artemis is called "the great goddess," and "the greatest goddess" (see Acts xix. 27). It is said in the twenty-ninth verse that "they rushed with one accord into the theatre," which seems strange, for in the Greek cities all public meetings were generally held in the market-place. But the inscriptions show that in Ephesus the great theatre was the place where all such meetings were held. The town clerk also is mentioned in the inscriptions, and it is clear that he was the keeper of the records of the city; it was his duty to see that the laws and edicts were inscribed on the walls or set up in a prominent place in the theatre. In verse thirty-nine mention is made of the "regular assembly," and the inscriptions show that this was the technical name of the mass meeting of the citizens which they held a certain number of times a year for the purpose of transacting business of various kinds; for the city was democratic in its form of government. On the walls of the very theatre in which this mass meeting was held was an inscription which defined robbery of the temple and various other acts as sacrilegious, and the town clerk could easily point to that and say, " These men are not guilty of sacrilege, they have never robbed the temple or blasphemed our goddess." Ephesus is also called " temple keeper of the great Artemis which fell down from heaven." " Temple keeper," we learn, was a title of honor, which might be assumed by any city that should build and support a temple for the worship of any particular god. So that Ephesus, since she had built the temple to Artemis, bore the honorary title of " temple keeper to the great Artemis." And in this temple, we know from other sources, was a very ancient statue representing the goddess, which was confidently believed to have fallen from heaven.

Our author has given us a good glimpse of the mob as the workmen were joined by the idlers on the street, all of whom caught up the cry, " Great is Artemis of the Ephesians." They all rushed into the theatre, but very few of them knew why they were shouting or what the cause of the demonstration was. It is a picture from life of a riotous crowd bent on mischief, without knowing why or to what purpose. The officials of the city were anxious to prevent any violence and to quiet the mob, for the city would be in danger of the charge of riot and illegal public meetings, and so might be deprived of some of her privileges or compelled to pay a heavy fine.

These three years at Ephesus were the most difficult and distressing of all Paul's life. They were far worse than the years of his imprisonment, galling as they must have been to his restless spirit. He recognized the great opportunities that Ephesus offered for missionary work, for he wrote to the Corinthians, "But I will tarry at Ephesus until Pentecost, for a great door and effectual is opened unto me," but he adds with great significance, "and there are many adversaries" (1 Cor. xvi. 9). His recollections of this have colored his words to the principal members of the church at Ephesus when he called them to come to Miletus to see him. He remembered it as a time of tears and of trials by the plots of the Jews. To this also refer the words in 2 Cor. i. 8–10: "For we would not have you ignorant, brethren, concerning our affliction which befell us in Asia, that we were weighed down exceedingly, beyond our power, insomuch that we despaired even of life: yea, we ourselves have had the answer of death within ourselves, that we should not trust in ourselves, but in God which raiseth the dead: who delivered us out of so great a death, and will deliver: on whom we have set our hope that he will also still deliver us." These words can have no other meaning than that in some way Paul had been brought face to face with a violent death from which he barely escaped. His death had seemed so certain that his escape seemed almost miraculous, and he attributed it to God. The sentence of death had been passed upon him, but God had delivered him. In Rom. xvi. 3-4 we have another of these mysterious references to some danger of death that had threatened to overtake him, but from which he had been delivered by the heroic action of Priscilla and Aquila, who had themselves risked their lives on his behalf. " Salute Priscilla and Aquila, my fellow-workers in Christ Jesus, *who for my life* laid down their own necks; unto whom not only I give thanks, but also all the churches of the Gentiles."

But we have a more explicit reference to one of the dangers that had befallen him. In 1 Cor. xv. 32 he says, " If after the manner of men I have fought with wild beasts at Ephesus, what doth it profit me?" This is not a mere figure of speech, as some have supposed; not at all. It means that Paul had actually been condemned to be thrown to the wild beasts in the amphitheatre. That was a common form of punishment, but not all who were thrown to the beasts were killed. It sometimes happened that they succeeded in killing the beast, and so they themselves escaped. Of course we cannot follow this out in the case of Paul, for unfortunately we know nothing of the details, but there can be no reasonable doubt that this was a part of his terrible experiences in these three years. It is interesting to note too that the second letter to the Corinthians, which was written just after the close of this period, is full of reminiscences of his sufferings. Read chapters iv., vi., and x. of this letter and see what his condition must have been. The life and death struggle in which he had been so long engaged had made an indelible impression on his mind, which is apparent in the whole epistle. His troubles still lay on him like a burden that oppressed and disquieted him.

His opponents were of three classes, the heathen, the Jews, and the Judaizers. We cannot follow them in all their machinations and violence, but we have seen how his life was endangered by the demonstration under Demetrius. The Jews were also assisting in this, for we find them putting forward Alexander to attack Paul and further increase the blind hatred of the populace. These facts, taken together with those above mentioned, the many adversaries, the sentence of death that had been passed upon him, the trials with the plots of the Jews, the circumstances that required Aquila and Priscilla to risk their lives for him, and his fighting with wild beasts, — what more is required to show that these three years were full of dangers and trials that would have conquered many another heart, however brave. What a light they throw on the zeal and devotion of Paul! The facts merely are given, leaving the imagination to supply the details.

But the Judaizers caused him even more anguish of heart, for they were endeavoring to destroy his life work, and more than once it seemed that they would succeed. They had before this begun to make systematic efforts to alienate the affections of his congregations from him. They sent out their missionaries everywhere on his track, sowing slanders of many kinds against him, and preaching another gospel; that is, they told his converts that they were not perfect Christians and that they could not hope to become partakers of the Messiah's kingdom until they had outwardly become Jews and observed the law of Moses. Everywhere they stirred up commotions, and threw the Gentile Christians into great perplexity, doubt, and distress of mind. Their arguments were plausible, their zeal great, and often they found ready credence. Where their success was not immediate they continued their efforts with such persistency, and were so shrewd in their arguments, and especially in the charges which they made against Paul, that in the end they were sure to prevail. And Paul found his congregations on all hands slowly deserting him and giving up his gospel of the freedom of salvation and of the right to the Messiah's kingdom through faith, and accepting the law of Moses, hoping by these observances to have a right to eternal life.

So that during these years he had to fight not only for his life against the heathen and Jews, but also for the life of his congregations and for the existence and preservation of his gospel. It is always sad when a man, who has spent the best years of his life in some great work and has seen his efforts crowned with success, is suddenly made aware that all his work is about to be undone, and is compelled to begin again, and, as it were, do the whole work over. The anxiety and anguish of mind are always touching in the extreme. How much more is this true of Paul, who saw his congregations falling away from him, his free gospel, his religion of the heart, displaced by the round of legal observances, and his own character traduced and all manner of false charges heaped upon him. He himself has given expression to the torture and distress of soul which he felt under the figure which to the ancients was the most expressive of pain; "My little children, of whom I am again in travail until Christ be formed in you." The struggle was a bitter one, and often Paul did not know on whose side the victory would be. It weighed upon him even more than the dangers that surrounded his person. For after speaking of the hardships which he had had to endure, the beatings and stonings, the shipwrecks, the fatiguing journeys, and the ever-present perils, he adds, "*Beside those things that are without, there is that which presseth upon me daily, anxiety for all the churches.*" This is wrung from him; it comes like a sob of pain from the depths of his heart. The perils, the physical dangers, that dogged his footsteps were as nothing compared with the anxiety of his soul as he saw the results of his years of labor about to be destroyed.

On his way to Ephesus in the year 54 he had passed through Galatia and even then had seen signs of the coming storm, and had warned the Galatians that those who received circumcision, hoping thereby to receive some spiritual advantage, were in reality bound to observe the whole Mosaic law; and he further pronounced a curse on all who should preach to them a gospel that differed from his own. But this had not had the desired effect, for soon after reaching Ephesus he heard that the Judaizers had been at least in part successful. Some of the Galatians had been persuaded by them to receive circumcision and were beginning to observe some of the Jewish feasts, regarding certain days and seasons as particularly holy, and thinking that they were pleasing God by such external observances. The Judaizers had made them believe that in order to become Christians they must first become Jews and accept at least a part of the Mosaic and levitical regulations as binding. They had further attempted to fortify their position by attacking Paul. For if they could succeed in discrediting him, it would of course be much easier to persuade his converts that his gospel was insufficient.

The charges were as follows: they declared that Paul was not on an equality with the other apostles, for he had not seen Jesus and had never received a commission from him to preach his gospel as the others had. His authority then was not equal to that of the Twelve, for they had theirs directly from Jesus. If Paul had any right at all to preach, he must have got it from some man or men. He was not an independent apostle; he had received all his knowledge of the Messiah and of his gospel from others. Since he is inferior in authority to the Twelve, in every question in which they differ they are to be accepted as supreme. What Paul says is to be corrected by what they say. Further, although he had got his gospel from them it was said that he had not preserved it in purity. He was no longer preaching the pure gospel as the others were, but he had corrupted it. He was no longer preaching the truth, but had changed it that he might please men. He was a coward and was not preaching for the truth's sake, but was using any means that seemed to promise success. Besides, he was covetous of fame and wealth, and was using his congregations to become famous and rich. It was a bitter attack on his apostleship, his gospel, and his character.

So he wrote his answer, his letter to the Galatians, — one of those fiery, indignant letters which must have made the Galatians wince more than once as they read it. He first takes up the question of his apostleship. He declares that he is an independent apostle and the equal of any, for he had his apostleship, not from men nor through any man, but directly from God through Jesus Christ. And for his gospel he was not indebted to any man, for no man taught it to him, or was in any way instrumental in giving it to him. But when Jesus had been revealed to him as the Messiah, it had all been made plain to him. He then reminds the Galatians that he had been so zealous for the law that he had most bitterly persecuted the Christians. But when it had pleased God to reveal his Son in him, to make known to him Jesus as the Messiah, he had at the same time been called to preach his gospel to the Gentiles. And immediately he had begun this. Without conferring with flesh and blood, without going up to Jerusalem to get the consent of the apostles, he went away to Arabia and at once entered upon the work to which he was called. So far from being dependent on the Twelve for his call to the apostleship and for his gospel and for the right to preach to the Gentiles, he had actually been for three years engaged in this before he even so much as saw one of the Twelve. It is clear from this that Paul must have been at work before he saw Peter, or his argument is worth nothing at all. If he had been simply meditating these three years in Arabia, if he had not been engaged in mission work, his opponents could easily overcome all he might say by simply calling attention to the fact that although he might claim to have been called by Christ, yet he did not begin his work until he had gone to Jerusalem to see Peter and get his permission to serve as a missionary. But that cannot be, for he proves the independence of his apostleship and of his gospel by saying that he began work at once, and had been three years in the field before he made the acquaintance of one of the Twelve. Besides, he had been with Peter only two weeks, and had seen no other apostle, but admits that he had seen James. From Jerusalem he went away into the regions of Syria and Cilicia, continuing his work, and remained unknown to the churches of Judæa and the other apostles until fourteen years after, when he went up to lay before them his gospel and his work.

With this he turns to another point. The independence of his apostleship and of his gospel is proved, but he must now show that the Twelve, or at least the representatives of the church at Jerusalem, have recognized him as their equal, that he had been intrusted with the gospel to the Gentiles, and that he was preaching a genuine gospel. So he refers to the conference which he had had with them about four or five years before. He and Barnabas had gone up to Jerusalem, taking with them Titus, who was a Greek. And he had laid before them his gospel, and showed them Titus as a sample of its fruits among the Gentiles. And although some of the Judaizers demanded that Titus be circumcised, regarding him with abhorrence since he was levitically unclean, yet Paul had resisted them and successfully opposed their demands, so that the apostles had not required his circumcision. They also made no addition to Paul's gospel; " they imparted nothing " to him, but they recognized that he was doing the Lord's work, for the Lord was with him. And since they saw that the grace of the Lord had been given him, they also strove against him no further, but gave him the right hand of fellowship. They stipulated, however, that he should go only to the Gentiles with his gospel, while they should continue with their gospel to the Jews. They made only one further request, namely, that Paul should remember the poor in Jerusalem.

But Paul has a still more convincing argument in the conduct of Peter at Antioch. For he had come down to Antioch and was so thoroughly agreed with Paul in all these things, that he associated freely with the uncircumcised Gentile Christians without any regard to the levitical law, thus by his conduct admitting that it was worthless, that it was no longer binding on either Jews or Gentiles and that its observance was a matter of entire indifference. He thus showed that there was complete agreement between himself and Paul. But here Paul tacitly admits that James did not agree with him, for he says that after " certain came from James," Peter, fearing the displeasure of James and the opposition of the Jewish Christians at Jerusalem, drew back from associating with the Gentiles. He feared to lose caste in Jerusalem, for he remembered that they had opposed him before when he had preached the gospel to Cornelius. But Paul publicly rebuked him, accusing him of hypocrisy because he knew that the law was not binding, and yet in order to have a good name with the Jewish party at Jerusalem he had acted contrary to his better knowledge and judgment.

With the third chapter he begins to discuss the relation existing between the law and the gospel. Abraham received the blessing simply because he believed God. The promise was made to him, not because he was keeping the law, but because he believed what God said to him. The great inheritance was promised him on this condition, and hence was for all who, like him, believed God. This promise God had confirmed by an oath. But four hundred and thirty years afterward God gave the law too to his descendants, but this could not annul the promise. For the inheritance had been made dependent simply on faith, and hence it could not now be made dependent on the observance of the law. The law had a different purpose, namely, to act as our tutor, to show us what sin is and lead us to Christ. But now that Christ is come we are no longer under this tutor, for Christ has revealed God as our Father, and through him we have received the adoption of sons, so that we are no longer bond-servants under the law but free sons of God.

But it by no means follows from the abolition of the law that we may indulge in sin. We are indeed free, but not free to sin, for a new principle of life has been implanted in us. We belong to God through Christ, and as his sons we must imitate Him. We must walk in his spirit, and become like Him in character. If we have the spirit of Christ we must produce the same fruits in our lives which he produced in his. "For the fruit of the Spirit is love, joy, peace, long-suffering, kindness, goodness, faithfulness, meekness, temperance; against such there is no law."

With the eleventh verse of the last chapter Paul begins to write the salutation with his own hand, for up to this point he has dictated and another has written. He tells them that these Judaizers have a special, selfish motive in persuading others to keep the law; it was that they, as Jewish Christians, might not be persecuted by their unbelieving brethren. It was that they might say that although they believed in Jesus, they were yet zealous for the law, and since they regarded it as the principal thing, they might thus recommend themselves to their Jewish brethren, and on this account escape the persecution that was falling upon other Christians.

And now he closes with the indignant words, "From henceforth let no man trouble me: for I bear branded on my body the marks of Jesus." He has spoken the last word; they may attack him if they choose, they may desert his gospel if they will, but let them trouble him no further, for he knows that he is the servant of Jesus. He bears on his body the marks of his apostleship. His back seamed by the rods of the Roman officers and the scourges of the Jewish authorities, and his body scarred by the stones of the mob at Lystra, were sufficient proofs to him of the genuineness of his apostleship, of the correctness of his gospel, and of the uprightness of his character. They may believe him or not, but he will not again condescend to defend himself against such base slanders.

The letter is severe, and written not without some hardness and bitterness (see especially v. 12), but it seems to have had the desired effect. For, a few months later, when writing to the Corinthians, he could inform them that the churches in Galatia were also taking part in the collection, and that the Christians at Corinth should follow the same method of making the collection as they. The crisis in Galatia was passed, and Paul had remained victor there; but the battle was yet to be waged all along the line. It was but the first skirmish, the prelude to a contest the end of which Paul himself was not to live to see.

Soon bad news came from the west. The church at Corinth was in a sad state. There were flagrant cases of fornication among the members. This sin, so frightfully common among the heathen, had polluted even the church. One of the members of the congregation had married his father's wife, that is, his stepmother. Whether she had been divorced or was a widow, it is not said, but the simple fact, under whatever circumstances, was an abomination, a pollution that could not be endured in the Christian community. In order to rebuke this and to put an end to it, Paul, as we learn from 1 Cor. v. 5, wrote them a letter telling them that Christians dare not associate with such. "I wrote you in my epistle to have no company with fornicators." His letter was disregarded. Apparently the transgressor was a man of influence, and the others, or at least some of them, did not wish to put him out of the congregation. So they pretended to misunderstand Paul's words. He had written that they should "have no company with fornicators." "Well, if that is the case," they said, "it will be necessary for us to go out of the world entirely. It is absolutely impossible to exist in the world and shun all such," and with this sham plea they excused themselves from acting against the one who had sinned in this way, and he remained as before, a member "in good standing." This letter of which Paul speaks and from which he quotes is lost. It is idle to speculate what the letter contained besides this. That the letter is lost need not be surprising, for it is not at all probable that we have all the letters that Paul and the other Apostles wrote. Does it seem likely that such a busy man as Paul, who founded so many churches and undoubtedly tried to keep in touch with as many of them as possible, should, in all the thirty years or more of his missionary activity, have written only a dozen letters? When we put the question in this way, the improbability of it is at once clear.

This lost letter to the Corinthians failed to accomplish its purpose; the guilty ones were not punished, but on the contrary the others were puffed up, as if, because they were Christians, they had the special right to allow such things to be practiced among them.

From comparison of Acts with 1 Corinthians we are able to determine the course of events as follows: This lost letter had no effect, but affairs in the congregation had grown worse in many ways. Under these circumstances Paul was visited in Ephesus by certain members of the household of Chloe, who were at the same time members of the neighboring church at Cenchreæ. These came bringing him an account of the condition of the rival church, which was divided into factions and parties (see 1 Cor. i. 11). Paul himself either could not or did not wish to go to Corinth, so he sent Timothy on a double errand. In the first place he should go with Erastus to Macedonia and arrange for the grand collection which he was already planning to take with him to Jerusalem, and then proceed to the south, to Corinth, and settle the difficulties there (1 Cor. iv. 7, xvi. 10, 11, Acts xix. 22). The way through Macedonia was of course much longer than by sea, and it would necessarily be some time before Timothy would reach Corinth.

But matters grew rapidly worse in the congregation. Several questions were being discussed, to which they could give no satisfactory answer, so they decided to ask Paul's advice. For this purpose they sent three men, Stephanus, Fortunatus, and Achaicus, with a letter to Paul, asking his opinion on several weighty matters which were before them. From this letter, and especially from the three men who had just come, Paul learned the exact condition of the church. In answer to their letter (which is lost), Paul wrote at once the letter which we call 1 Corinthians and sent it the short way, by the sea, expecting that it would reach Corinth before the arrival of Timothy (1 Cor. xvi. 10, 11).

Let us now turn to the letter itself, and see what the condition of the church was. The first thing we learn is, that the church was divided into parties because of personal preferences for the various leading missionaries that had been among them. It lay in the character of the Greeks to form parties and cliques. They had a strong social instinct, and could not live apart from others. This led him to develop what we may call a most vigorous club-life. They had an almost infinite number of clubs, guilds, associations, and societies of all kinds. It was the misfortune of the Greeks that they never could agree. It was this spirit of contention that ruined Greece. It appeared in everything, not only in their political life, in trade, and handicraft, but also in their schools of philosophy and rhetoric. The students of one professor jostled and hooted those of another in the street, and often there were broken heads and bloody faces when they came into too close quarters. The Greek gave his whole self to the cause that he espoused or to the opinion that he adopted, with the necessary consequence that he was always in a clique with those who agreed with him, and in bitter strife with those who differed from him.

This national habit or characteristic showed itself in the church at Corinth. Some of them were devoted admirers of Paul and of his way of presenting the truth. They preferred him because of his manner, or because of his teachings. They had probably caught up some of his peculiar words and phrases which pleased them, and which seemed to express the truth better than any other form of words. But others preferred Apollos. He had come among them, a skilled philosopher and rhetorician; thoroughly trained in the schools, and able by the skill with which he arranged and clothed his ideas to impress and please those who had great æsthetic pleasure in such things. His teaching had been cast in a philosophical mould; he had had much to say of "knowledge" and "wisdom;" he had used the technical terms that were in use in the philosophical schools, and these had made a great impression on his hearers, who were thus delighted with the learning of the man, and fancied that they had arrived at a higher stage of truth through his instruction than through that of Paul.

It has already been said that the Greeks laid all emphasis on knowledge. That was the principal thing, for virtue consisted in knowledge, not in the condition of the heart and character. So these Greeks at Corinth were especially pleased with Apollos and his form of teaching, because it seemed to fall in with their ideas about the importance and value of philosophical knowledge and speculation. Their knowledge and conception of Christianity were so superficial, that Christ was nothing, his ministers everything. To correct this false impression Paul takes up the first four chapters of this letter with a contrast between the gospel and philosophy. The teaching of Christ is not a philosophy, and it is not to be compared with any of the Greek systems. It is not the wisdom for which the Greek so longs, but is something quite different. The gospel is the sure news which Christ has brought, that there is a God who is the Father of all; that He is gracious and merciful to his children, and has shown his attitude towards them and his affection for them in the person of Jesus, who died for them; and whom He raised from the dead to a position of power, thus putting a seal upon his work and teaching, that all might trust Him, and as children of God walk worthily of their high position.

Paul admits that he had been tempted to try the philosophical form for his teaching, for that would have pleased the Greek taste, but then he had determined to preach the simple gospel; to know nothing among them but Christ crucified, for Christ is shown to be the power and wisdom of God, in the new motives and impulses, and consequently in the new life, which we have from and through him. But Paul further excuses himself for not having used this form of teaching, because the Corinthians had not yet learned the rudiments of Christianity; they were still babes; they were carnal. To be spiritually minded, to have the mind of Christ, was to walk as Christ walked, in purity of life and character, without jealousy and strife; it was to be like Christ, pleasing God by keeping our hearts pure, and by doing the duties which we owe Him and others. If they had reached this stage, then they might speculate if they chose, but until they had learned the one all-important thing, it was impossible for him to proceed beyond the simple truths of the gospel. This is the gospel. Others may build further, but let each one see how he builds. This truth in Christ is the essential thing; it is Christianity. It stands secure. But the work of each one, that is, the further additions and speculations of each, shall be tried. One may have built well, may have found out much truth and been thereby helpful to others; all such shall receive a reward. Another may have gone entirely wrong in what he has thought and said; his further philosophical speculations may be all false, but if he has left the foundation truth untouched, although his work shall perish he shall not himself miss the kingdom of God.

In fact, it is necessary that each should be an independent worker and builder on this foundation, for each has his own work. Each is a steward, and a steward must be found faithful in the management and development of that intrusted to him. Paul had expressed the truth as God had given it to him; all that he is he has received from God. Apollos had his own way of teaching, but he too had received everything from God. They could not agree absolutely in everything, for they were two individuals, two personalities, and every personality received its peculiar characteristics and distinctions from God. The spirit speaks through these. It must not be expected that all shall say the same things in the same way. But each must be faithful to God, to himself, and to the truth which God gave him to see. Paul himself had come to the Corinthians, not with the words of wisdom, but with this simple gospel which to the learned seemed foolishness, but with it he had laid the foundation. That is, he had given them a knowledge of the essential truth. But Apollos had come, and, in a different way, built further, but had not destroyed the foundation or laid another one.

In all this he has been carrying on a gentle rebuke to the Corinthians. He has been thinking all the time of Apollos and himself, for he says: "Now these things, brethren, I have in a figure transferred to myself and Apollos for your sakes; that in us ye might learn not to go beyond the things that are written, that no one of you be puffed up for the one against the other." That is, "the differences between Apollos and me are not so great as you have imagined, for you have attributed too much weight and importance to the form of the teaching and to the secondary truths which you have learned from him. I gave you all the essential truth of Christianity. That is sufficient, but if you make further speculations let them not be pressed into differences and made causes for division. Above all, personal preferences should have no such influence. For what is Apollos, and what is Paul? Only servants, who served each with the gifts which God had given him, for which each shall receive his peculiar reward."

Knowing the great value attributed by the Greeks to knowledge, and the constant danger to which they were exposed in this direction, with chapter iii. 18 he begins a brief warning against the "wisdom of this world;" and by that he means undoubtedly the speculations about the many questions which were agitating the minds of men, and were discussed with such subtlety by the philosophers. They were questions about the substance of the world, its nature and essence, its origin, its destiny, about the mysteries of life and death, and the thousand and one other questions that come to every one who stops to observe and think about the things that are about him. These things are foolishness if they are thought to be religious or if put into the place of religion, for they are knowledge which shall be done away. But the true wisdom is the knowledge of God which has been revealed through Christ, and if they possess that they possess all things.

Instead of striving about who is the greatest, they ought rather to rejoice in the possession of all things, since no matter what the explanation of the mysteries of the world, of life and death; no matter what the course of things may bring forth, they are safe in the keeping of Christ, and he is safe in the keeping of God. But instead of this childlike trust in God, this leaving everything to his fatherly care, they had been puffed up as if they owed Him nothing; as if they had filled themselves and made themselves rich. They had forgotten their position as servants, and had assumed the place of rulers; they had forgotten the humble position which Paul occupied, and were not following his example. And then in a few sharp sentences and with the finest irony he reminds them of his condition, and contrasts it with their high pretensions. They had forgotten him, their spiritual father, and were reigning without him. He had had no share in their glory. But no, you have not really reigned, but, " I would that ye did reign, that I also might reign with you. For I think God hath set forth us the apostles last of all, as men doomed to death: for we are made a spectacle unto the world, and to angels, and to men. We are fools for Christ's sake, but ye are wise in Christ; we are weak, but ye are strong; ye have glory, but we have dishonor. Even unto this present hour we both hunger, and thirst, and are naked, and are buffeted, and have no certain dwelling-place; and we toil, working with our own hands: being reviled, we bless; being persecuted, we endure; being defamed, we intreat: we are made as the filth of the world, the offscouring of all things, even until now" (iv. 8–13). This was Paul's condition, although he was an apostle. Let the Corinthians remember that the time is not yet come for reigning. It is the time for serving and suffering, for doing the work that God has given to each.

But there was also a party in Corinth which preferred Peter. From the fact that there were such, it is almost certain that Peter had also been in Corinth in the mean time, though probably only for a short time, and some had thought him greater than either Apollos or Paul.

They were saying, "I am of Paul," and "I am of Apollos," and "I am of Peter," but Paul in a single sentence administers the sharpest rebuke possible, for he adds, "I am of Christ, yet you, by your cliques, divide Christ. Has Paul been crucified for you?"

There was also the beginning of another party, which later was to develop into a strong, violent opposition to Paul. Some of them were puffed up, and were saying that Paul did not dare come to Corinth.

It must be noted that in all this discussion about Apollos, Peter, and himself, there is nothing that would indicate that there was any opposition existing among themselves. He speaks of Apollos in terms of the highest recognition, and there is not a word of blame or detraction against either him or Peter. On the contrary, the language used of Apollos in chapter xvi. 12 shows that Paul and Apollos were on the most friendly terms, for Paul wished Apollos to return to Corinth to help settle the difficulties that were troubling the congregation. But Apollos had evidently had enough of the Corinthians and was greatly displeased with their conduct. For, although Paul had begged him to return, he had persistently and determinedly refused. But still Paul hoped that he would come at some future time.

In the fifth chapter he turns to the flagrant case of fornication, and demands that the whole congregation shall meet and solemnly expel the offender, and that they shall refuse to readmit him to their society or fellowship until he has repented. More than that, they must have no fellowship with fornicators, with covetous, with idolators, with revilers, with extortioners. For the church must consist of those who have ceased to practice such abominations and are striving to imitate the conduct of Christ, and to live according to the laws of the kingdom of God.

There was further a lack of Christian brotherly love among them. They quarreled with each other, and were having lawsuits, and, although they were Christian brethren, they appealed to heathen judges to settle their difficulties (vi. 1–11). It was a great defect in them that they had such differences at all. Why not rather suffer wrong? Why not rather submit to being defrauded? For that certainly is more in keeping with the teaching and example of Christ, than that they should themselves defraud and wrong others. Above all, they should by no means appeal to the heathen to decide between them, but rather let some Christian brother settle their strifes.

Again he turns to the question of fornication (vi. 12). The whole defect was that they did not look upon this as a sin. Especially among the Greeks, the view was prevalent that lust was a natural appetite, just like hunger and thirst, and that the satisfying of the one was as innocent as that of the other. As the belly is for meats and meats for the belly, so the body is for fornication. So far from being a sin, it was even looked upon as a part of the worship of some of the gods. But Paul reminds them that there is a world-wide difference between them, for fornication is a defilement of the body, which is the temple of the Holy Spirit.

With the seventh chapter Paul begins to answer certain questions which they had asked him in the letter which the three brethren had brought with them. The question of marriage and the marriage duty was agitating them. They were not clear whether marriage was right or not, and the mutual rights and duties of husband and wife were in controversy. The question was still more perplexing if the husband or wife were an unbeliever. Was it not necessary that the Christian husband or wife should be separated from his unbelieving partner?

Paul says in reply, "It is a good thing not to marry; I say unto the unmarried and widows, it is good for them that they abide even as I," that is, unmarried. But all do not have the gift of continence, and therefore, that temptation and sin may be avoided, it is better that each man have his own wife and each woman her own husband. For the married state is not sinful, but is in accordance with the will and arrangements of God. But if the unbelieving partner is unwilling to continue the marriage relation with a Christian, let no force be used to compel him to do so, for the Christian wife or husband thus deserted is without fault or blame.

Since circumcision was not of any religious value, some of the Jewish Christians were endeavoring by artificial means to remove the mark of circumcision, which among the Greeks was a sign of barbarism and was looked upon with disgust. Others, on the contrary, were receiving it as if it were of value. To these, Paul says, both are wrong, for there is no value in either circumcision or uncircumcision. The one thing is to do the will of God by performing faithfully the duties of our calling.

With the preaching of the gospel and the brotherhood of believers, the question of slavery at once arose, and might at any moment become a burning one. If a slave is a free man in Christ, and the brother of his master, can it be right for him to remain in the position of a slave? Ought he not rather to insist on being set free and in all things recognized as the equal of his master? Paul's answer is, No, each one should remain in the occupation in which Christianity found him. Christianity is not to bring about a revolution; it is not to overthrow the social and economic system by violent measures. On the contrary, it is to sanctify and ennoble every honest calling, every duty, and all the relations of life. Religion has nothing to do with the external or social condition, but each should remain where the gospel found him. For the slave is a free man in Christ, and the free man is a slave in Christ, for all are brethren by the law of Christ.

In the matter of marriage and in the giving or withholding of a daughter in marriage, Paul gives his own judgment, his opinion, for he says that Christ left no command in regard to those things. He lays it upon them, not as a command, but as his opinion. It is what his "sanctified commonsense" tells him is right. Remain as you are; if married, seek not a divorce; if unmarried, seek not a partner; but if you do marry, you have committed no sin. But the time is short, we are in the last days, and we ought to be careful for the things of the Lord, and to be ready for what is coming. But he who marries, assumes duties and relations which must necessarily hinder him from being so careful for the things of the Lord as he might otherwise be. According to the customs of those times, the father had the sole right to dispose of his daughter's hand in marriage. Paul found no fault with this, but said that each father should act in this matter as seemed good to him. If he chose to give his daughter in marriage, it was good, if not, however, it was better; for Paul believed that because of the "present distress" and of the "shortness of the times" she would be happier unmarried, for she would thereby escape much tribulation in the flesh.

In the eighth chapter he answers their question about meats that had been sacrificed to idols. It was the custom to offer an animal in sacrifice in the temple, have the flesh prepared, and invite one's friends to take part in this temple meal. The Corinthian Christians were at a loss to know whether they might accept such an invitation, or whether they might under any circumstances partake of such flesh. Paul says in answer: Of course you know that these idols are nothing; there is but one God, who has made, controls, and knows all things. You know that eating of itself has nothing to do with religion; you can neither please nor displease God thereby. It is perfectly proper to accept such an invitation, for you would eat of this flesh as coming from God's hand; you would eat it to his glory. But some one who does not have this knowledge may see you seated in a heathen temple taking part in one of these temple meals. He would regard this as a sin, and would be offended at it; or he might think that he might do the same thing, and so would take part in such a meal as if it were really a sacrifice to another god, and thus bring upon himself the guilt of idolatry. So that, although you have a right to take part in such meals, yet if you thereby wound the weak conscience of a brother, or lead him to fall into sin, you should deny yourselves of the privilege. If need be, you should abstain wholly from such meals.

But some went further, and said that it was perfectly proper for the Christian to go through the motions of offering sacrifice. They know that these idols are nothing, and can therefore perform these rites without being guilty of idolatry. But here Paul draws the line. The idols to which the heathen sacrifice are, to be sure, not gods, but they are demons, evil spirits, and if we offer them sacrifices, we thereby show that we wish to have communion with them. But we cannot have fellowship with these and at the same time with Christ. And again Paul repeats what he has said in the eighth chapter: these things are lawful, each one has the abstract right to practice them, but there is a higher power that may forbid it. Each one is bound to build up, to strengthen, his fellow-Christians. He must do nothing which will cause another to stumble. Therefore if you are invited to a feast, and choose to accept, go and eat what is set before you without asking any questions, for you give thanks to God, the Giver of all. But if some Christian brother with a weak conscience tells you that this flesh has been offered to idols, you must abstain from eating, lest you wound his conscience and lead him into sin. For in all things we must imitate Christ, who sought not his own pleasure, but came to serve.

Paul had asserted the high principle, that in Christ there is neither Jew nor Gentile, neither bond nor free, neither male nor female. That is, all are on an equality. It follows necessarily from this that slaves ought to be free and that women should have equal rights with the men. That is just the conclusion which some of the slaves were making, as we have seen from 1 Cor. vii. 21, and now we learn that the women had begun to act on this logical inference. They appeared in the meetings of the Christians, and took part in the worship, praying and prophesying with uncovered heads, that is, with unveiled faces. They thought Christianity was to produce a revolution in the social customs, and free them from all the limitations that were to them, no doubt, very burdensome. This new-found liberty and equality were to be used to the full, regardless of the consequences. But such conduct was contrary to all of the world's conceptions of modesty and proper conduct on the part of women. It was exceedingly offensive to every one. If this should be identified as a part of Christian teaching and principle, it would cause a total misconception of the essential character of Christianity, and bring about opposition, contempt, and ridicule. So, of course, Paul opposes it. But his arguments are drawn wholly from the universal sense of propriety. He indeed says that the woman was created for the man, and not the man for the woman, but he at once deprives this of all weight, by saying that the man without the woman is nothing, even as also the woman without the man. He says, too, that the woman ought to have authority on her head because of the angels, but what Paul meant by that no one now knows. Further than this he could only add, " Does not nature, that is, your sense of propriety, tell you that the woman ought to have her head covered ? " But here he does not criticise the woman for taking part in the services, but only because they did so with the head uncovered. But in 1 Cor. xiv. 34 he returns to the question, and forbids the women to speak in the church because it is regarded as improper; it is contrary to public opinion !

Paul, with the ninth chapter, turns to his personal opponents, to refute them and defend himself against their false charges. From this we learn something of their opposition to him, and the charges which they made against him. They too had denied his apostleship ; he had not seen Christ as the other apostles had. He was not a free, independent apostle as the Twelve were. But Paul replies, " although I may not be regarded as an apostle by others, yet I certainly am an apostle to you, for I preached Christ to you." His success was sufficient proof of his apostleship. This was his defense to those who attacked his authority. They had further said that the reason Paul had not received money from his churches was that he had no right to do so. They knew it was his custom always to work to support himself, and they declared that he had made a virtue out of necessity, and had pretended to do so from choice. No, he was not a free genuine apostle, equal to the others; they might receive support from their churches, but he had no such right. They even made capital out of the fact that the other apostles were married and Paul was not. In some way this was explained to his disadvantage. Both Paul and Barnabas were attacked in this way.

But Paul defends himself and Barnabas with several arguments. No soldier ever serves at his own expense; no man plants a vineyard without having a right to eat of its fruit; no man feeds a flock without having the right to the milk which it produces; even God had provided that no one should work for others without being supported by them, since he had commanded that even the ox should not be muzzled while he was at work, but should be allowed to have his share of the grain which he had helped to till and thresh. Besides, Paul had brought them spiritual possessions, which are of far more value than temporal goods: had he not the right to receive the smaller in return for the greater? Since he had been the first to bring them the truth, had he not a greater right than those who came after him? Further, it is the rule, the world over, that those who minister in sacred things, and are connected with a temple, should live from the gifts to the temple. But he has even a still higher authority, for Christ himself had declared that those who went out to proclaim his gospel should live thereby. But while Paul knew that this was his right, he had not used it. He had determined to make the gospel free, that it might be clear to all that his motives were pure, and that he was preaching, not for the sake of the gain, but because of his love and devotion to Christ. He had not used all of his rights, but had denied himself in many ways. Although free from the observance of the law of Moses, he had yet lived as though bound by it, in order that he might win those who were still under it. To the heathen who were without the law of Moses he had shown that he also was without that law, but that he was under the law of Christ, the law of love and service, that he might win these for Christ. Let no one suppose that this was easy for him to do; by no means, for it is a hard struggle, and it is necessary for him to buffet his body and bring it into subjection. It is a duty laid upon him, and it is necessary that he be found faithful, or he may lose his reward, and himself be rejected. From 2 Corinthians we learned that this party was not silenced by this defense, but the opposition continued until it reached its climax, and led to a sharp crisis in the congregation, as we shall see when we come to speak of that later.

The passage 1 Cor. xi. 17–34, shows us a strange picture of the affairs in the church and especially of the way in which the Lord's supper was celebrated. In the first place, they carried their party strifes and divisions even into this. It was the custom for all the members to bring food with them to the place of meeting, and all was then put together and a meal prepared of which all were to eat without any distinction. Then, at a convenient moment, probably at the end of the meal, reference was made to the sufferings and death of Jesus, and all partook of the bread and wine. Thus it formed the close of a greater meal, just as on the night of its institution it formed the close of the passover meal. But in Corinth the members were divided into cliques, and even this meal was no longer a common one, for some had an abundance and others had nothing. By some it was made an occasion of feasting and drinking, while others even suffered hunger. It was impossible, therefore, for them to observe the Lord's supper. It had been instituted as a common meal, a symbol of the Christian equality and brotherhood, but they were making it a mark of division.

The chapters twelve to fourteen are taken up with the discussion of what is called spiritual gifts. The conception on which this is based is as follows: Every Christian has the Spirit, which inspires him, or leads him to do what he can for the general or particular welfare of the congregation, or of the whole body of Christians. This activity, of whatever kind, was regarded as a gift of the Spirit. Some were apostles, others were prophets, others were teachers, others could work miracles or powers (but we are nowhere told what these were); others spoke with tongues, others could interpret these, others had the "word of wisdom or knowledge," that is, they could give satisfactory answers to the many deep, dark questions which were then disturbing the minds of men; others had the gift of serving in various ways, the gift of liberality, mercy, hospitality, and so forth. Thus every activity in the congregation was regarded as a gift of the Spirit. Each one therefore, according to his ability, which was his gift, worked for the welfare of all. Some services were, of course, in the eyes of men more honorable than others, but all were necessary. And just as there can be no jealousy and strife between the various members of the body, so there ought to be none between the members of Christ's body, all of whom are thus inspired by the same spirit. But some might profess to be Christians, to have the Spirit, and yet be wrong, and deceive others. How were these to be tested? How could one guard against this danger? There are two tests to be applied to all who claim to have the spirit. In the first place, we must ask, "What is your attitude to the person of Jesus?" No one who opposes Jesus or sets himself above him has the Spirit. Such a one is false and must not be trusted. The other test is the one which Jesus himself gave, "By their fruits ye shall know them;" that is, by their manner of life. If they follow the principles which Christ taught, if they exhibit an undisturbed trust in God, if they deny themselves by doing their duty, rather than seeking their own pleasure, and if they serve others in love; in a word, if they imitate Jesus in their daily lives, they have the Spirit of God and are to be listened to.

Now what was the trouble at Corinth? Everything had fallen into disorder because, in a spirit of strife and pride, each one insisted that his gift was the most important of all, and that when he had anything to say the others must keep still. Their meetings, instead of being orderly and becoming, had become a bedlam of confusion and contention, each demanding that he be heard, and refusing to give place to another.

One gift especially seems to have been cultivated almost to the exclusion of others. They were seized with a kind of craze for it, and esteemed it above all others in value and importance. They looked upon the speaking of tongues as far more important and honorable than the simple preaching of the word. There was a showiness and mystery about this which attracted all and made them despise other gifts. The mysterious ecstacy of the speaker, the strange influence of the Spirit, the "unknown tongue," all were looked upon with honor and envy, although the message was seldom understood. And so taken up were they with this, that they each strove to surpass the other, and boasted of their much speaking. They would estimate a man's goodness and dignity by the amount of this power which he possessed, while the one who wished to speak a plain word for their edification was scarcely allowed the time for such a commonplace act. But Paul rebukes them for this, because they are measuring everything by a false standard. They look simply at the externals, at that which is calculated to fill one with awe and admiration. He then gives them the true standard for measuring the value of all these gifts. He lays down the principle that that gift is highest and most valuable which brings the greatest profit to the greatest number; that gift is lowest and of least value which benefits the smallest number. Speaking with tongues was showy, but it helped no one except its possessor, because generally no one else could understand it. That it could be helpful to others, it was necessary that it be interpreted. Consequently it was one of the lowest and least valuable gifts. The working of wonders is put very low too, because it affects only a few. The gift of prophesying, of preaching, of instruction in the way of the Lord, of exhortation, is of very great value, because it benefits almost the whole congregation.

They should all, therefore, desire the greater spiritual gifts, those by which they would be most serviceable to the whole body of Christians. But is it not impossible for all to have the greater gifts? No, for the greatest gift is in the reach of all; the gift, too, without which all other gifts are entirely valueless. So Paul shows them a still more excellent way in that grand lyric of Christian love (ch. xiii.) whose teaching has never yet been adequately exemplified in the life of the Christian church. The power to speak with all tongues, of both men and angels, all the power of prophecy, the knowledge of all mysteries, the power to work miracles, the greatest liberality, the greatest self-sacrifice, without love, are nothing (vss. 4-7).

Prophecies and tongues and theological speculations are imperfect; they are connected with the limitations that now hem us in. But when the perfect time comes they shall all cease. But love shall never end. It is greater than all other gifts, even than faith and hope. For faith and hope, although of the utmost importance, are individual, they affect directly and principally only their possessors. But love affects all, indeed, it is essential to the very existence of the church. It is the family affection, without which Christians cannot recognize each other as brethren. It is that which binds all together and makes each one willing to spend himself in the service of others. The point of view from which everything is to be looked at and judged is that of the whole church and not that of the individual. From this point of view love is the greatest of all. Not the love that consists in a theoretical enthusiasm for humanity in general, and exhausts itself in writing æsthetic essays about the dignity and nobility of man, but a feeling of sympathy translated into action, into a life of service and helpfulness for others. And this inestimable gift is in the reach of all, for every one can serve his brethren with all his powers. "He that would be greatest in the kingdom of heaven, let him be the servant of all."

In the fifteenth chapter Paul discusses the resurrection. Some in Corinth had denied that there is such a thing as the resurrection of the dead, and that not even Jesus made an exception to this rule. Paul refutes this, first, by reminding them that it was an essential part of his gospel that Jesus had been raised from the dead. He names those to whom he had appeared, first to Peter, then to the Twelve, then to more than five hundred brethren at once, many of whom were still alive and could testify to the fact; then to James, and again to all the first disciples, and last of all to himself. Paul bases everything on the resurrection of Christ; if he was not raised then we have no assurance that we shall be raised. But the fact stands secure, that the Christ still lives. The testimony for it cannot be doubted. The proofs are overwhelming.

Mocking, they had asked, " but with what kind of body shall the dead be raised ? Shall these bodies which we now have be restored ? " They could form no clear idea of what the resurrection body would be, and therefore the resurrection seemed to them impossible. In the first place, we must not think that we shall be raised with these bodies, for flesh and blood cannot inherit the kingdom of God. And then Paul uses a comparison, the point of which has been generally overlooked. A seed of wheat, for instance, is cast into the ground, quickens, and dies, but from it there springs up, not another grain of wheat, but a stalk of different form or body, but such as God has appointed to it. So also of the resurrection body. The body which we now have is weak, inglorious, corruptible, natural. But it is laid away and "dies," and as the form of the plant differs from that of the seed, so the form of the resurrection body shall differ from that of the body that is laid away. But God will give to each the proper form. What it will be, we do not know. We can only say of it that it will be incorruptible, glorious, not subject to weakness, spiritual. For Jesus has become a life-giving spirit, and we shall be like him. Although we have now the image of the earthly, we shall bear the image of the heavenly; for Jesus has made it possible for us to become partakers of the divine nature.

In the last chapter he gives them directions about making the collection for the Church at Jerusalem. On the first day of the week each should lay by him in store, as he has prospered during the week. Paul does not yet know whether he shall go to Jerusalem with this collection, or send it by messengers. He promises to come to them after he has passed through Macedonia, for it is his intention to make a tour through that province. His further movements are, as yet, uncertain. He may even spend the next winter in Corinth, but excuses himself for not coming to them at once, on the ground that he could remain with them but a short time, and he does not wish to see them simply "by the way," but wishes to "tarry a while with them." For the present, therefore, he will remain in Ephesus, for he is in the midst of great opportunities.

There is no mention of any church officers, no deacons and elders. We learn only that the members of the house of Stephanas *have set themselves* to minister unto the saints; that is, to manage the affairs of the congregation and attend to the various needs of the church. They had set themselves to do this, for this, too, was a gift and not an office. Such devotion deserves recognition. Let the Corinthians show them, and all others who engage in this work, the proper respect and due reverence.

What the effect of the letter was we can only infer. Apparently it accomplished its purpose, for in the second letter nothing is said about any of these questions. It failed, however, in one point. It did not quiet the opponents of Paul. On the contrary, their opposition increased to such a pitch that he thought it best to make a journey directly to Corinth without waiting to go through Macedonia. He hoped by going in person to be able to silence them, to secure thereby the recognition of his apostleship and the deference due him, and to restore peace to the congregation. We know of this visit only from the second letter to the Corinthians. In chapter ii. 1 he says, " But I determined this for myself, that I would not come again to you with sorrow." That is, he had already come to them once with sorrow; but that certainly cannot apply to the stay of eighteen months during his first missionary journey. In xii. 14 he says, " Behold, this is the *third* time I am ready to come to you," and in xiii. 1, " this is the *third* time I am coming to you," and xiii. 2, " I have said beforehand, and I do say beforehand, as when I was present the *second* time." Evidently, therefore, some time after the writing of 1 Corinthians he made a visit to Corinth. But this visit was by no means a success. The opponents had been very bold, and he had not been able to silence them. He had made a very poor impression on them. He had written in the first letter that he was coming to them shortly and he would know " not the word of them which are puffed up, but the power." And unfortunately that is just what he did "know," for they were too strong for him. They now had ground to say that his letters were violent and blustering, and full of threats, but if he came in person he was weak and contemptible and could do nothing by his words. They had successfully resisted him, and almost the whole congregation had either agreed with them or at least were very cold in their support of him. Under these circumstances Paul left Corinth and went up into Macedonia, intending to return again to Corinth and from there to go to Jerusalem. But after reaching Macedonia he changed his mind and determined not to go back to Corinth. This, also, led to the charge of fickleness ; he was a man who did not know his own mind (i. 15–17). He now explains this charge. He had not returned because he wished to avoid the " scene " that must necessarily follow between him and his opponents. He had come to them with sorrow once, he would not do so again. The Corinthians had not treated him as they should. His opponents were bitter. If he should return, he must rebuke them severely. He must overcome them.

This would be too painful for them, as well as for himself. So he determined to spare them. Instead of returning to Corinth he wrote them another letter (a third), sharp, severe, which would "cause sorrow." "For though I made you sorry with my epistle, I do not regret it, though I did regret; for I see that that epistle made you sorry, though but for a season." "For behold, this selfsame thing, that ye were made sorry after a godly sort, what earnest care it wrought in you, yea, what clearing of yourselves, yea, what indignation, yea, what fear, yea, what longing, yea, what zeal, yea, what avenging! In everything ye approved yourselves to be pure in the matter" (vii. 8-11).

"For out of much affliction and anguish of heart I wrote unto you with many tears; not that ye should be made sorry, but that ye might know the love which I have more abundantly unto you" (ii. 4). Such language cannot refer to 1 Corinthians, for there is nothing in that letter which would justify such words.

Evidently in this letter he told them the plain truth. It was a letter that would bring about a crisis. They must either right the wrong they had done him, rebuke his opponents and stand squarely upon his side, or they must break entirely with him. There could no longer be any half-way measures. They must decide either for or against him.

This letter he sent by Titus to Corinth, but he himself returned to Asia, perhaps to Ephesus; but his anxiety was so great that he soon went to Troas, hoping there to meet Titus with an answer from the Corinthians. And although " a door was opened unto him in the Lord " he had no relief for his spirit, because Titus was not there (ii. 12). He could not endure the suspense. He feared that the Corinthians had entirely deserted him. So he went over into Macedonia again, hoping to meet Titus there, but still he had not come. His anxiety increased. He was afflicted on all sides; without were fightings, within were fears. He wished he had not written them so sharply. He could not endure it if the Corinthians should cast him off and go with his opponents. The suspense was intolerable. But at last Titus came with good news. The majority of the congregation had, at the critical moment, been faithful to him. They now longed for him, they mourned that they had offended him, they showed great zeal for him. They had cleared themselves of all blame, by punishing the principal offender. The opposition to him was put down; it no longer ruled, although some still bitterly opposed him (vi. 11–13, and vii. 2–16).

Filled with joy at this news, Paul now wrote a fourth letter to the Corinthians (our 2 Cor.), which is hearty, tender, and thankful, except the last four chapters, which deal with those who still opposed him. This letter he sent to Corinth by Titus, who was accompanied by two other brethren (viii. 16–22).

Turning to the letter itself, we see, first of all, that it was only the majority of the congregation that had been true to him, and even their support was not as hearty and as enthusiastic as he desired. For they had acknowledged him only in part (i. 14). He begs them to lay aside their coldness to him; his heart is enlarged toward them. They are not straitened in him, but they are straitened in their own affections; let them repay him by enlarging their hearts toward him (vi. 11–13). Again he begs them to open their hearts to him, for he had not wronged any of them; he had taken advantage of none of them; they are "in his heart to die together and live together" (vii. 2–4). In viii. 24 he begs them to receive Titus and the two brethren who are representatives of other churches in such a way as to show them that they really love him and are true to him. He is careful to tell them all the good things he has been saying about them; among other things he has been boasting to the Macedonians that the Corinthians have been ready with their contributions for a year. Throughout the letter there are traces of this effort on the part of Paul to smooth over all the difficulties and make them forget all the late unpleasantness. That he is still under its shadow, however, and that he feels that he is treading on dangerous ground, is apparent from the fact that he more than once corrects himself, after appearing to have given a command, and says that he does not mean to give them orders, but that he seeks the proof of their love. Thus in the eighth chapter he tells them to be sure to abound in the grace of giving, for he wishes to take a large collection to Jerusalem; but lest they should be offended and say that he was assuming authority over them, he at once says, "I speak not by way of commandment, but as proving, through the earnestness of others, the sincerity also of your love."

If we ask who were the originators of this trouble in Corinth, we learn that they were not original members of the church, but had come from some other place, fortified with letters of recommendation (iii. 1). They claimed to have the truth in a direct way from Jesus, and apparently laid stress on the fact, either that they had seen him, or that they were authorized by some one who had stood very near to him while on earth (x. 7).

In answer to this Paul says that it is not the Christ as He was in the flesh, but the Christ that lives, having been raised from the dead, that has all power and is of decisive importance.

They were undoubtedly members of the party that was so zealous for the law. They had begun their work in Corinth by attacking Paul, hoping in this way to make the introduction of the law easy. The size and activity of this party may be inferred from Paul's language in chap. ii. 17, "we are not as the *many*, corrupting the word of God." According to

Paul's own admission this party in the church was then in the majority.

But besides these "foreigners," there was especially one member of the congregation who had made common cause with them, and had even surpassed them in violence and bitterness against Paul (ii. 5–11). There had evidently been a violent encounter between them. Paul felt himself greatly injured by this one, and in his letter demanded that they punish the offender. This they had done. But as he had repented, they had forgiven him, and Paul says that he also forgives him, and that the penitent one should now be restored.

But Paul hints at other opponents, who had been guilty of grave moral offenses, and who had been unwilling to submit to the censures which he had passed upon them. For in xii. 20–21, and xiii. 2 he fears that he shall find strife, jealousy, wraths, factions, backbiting, whisperings, swellings, tumults, and that he will be compelled to mourn over those who have sinned and have not heeded his warnings and threats.

The charges against him were many and various. They said he was fickle, changeable, and never knew his own mind (i. 17). No attention was to be paid to him, for he was "out of his head," he was beside himself (v. 13); he was rude in speech, as much as to say, " he is no preacher " (xi. 6); his letters were violent and threatening, but he was quite harmless and meek when he came in person (x. 1 and 10). One of their charges had especially offended Paul; they said he was a boaster, a braggart, always praising and bragging about himself. That cut him to the quick. He is continually referring to it in this letter. Whenever he has said anything about himself, he at once says, "Do you think I am boasting and commending myself again?" (iii. 1, v. 12, x. 18). This hurt and hemmed him all the time, till finally (xi. 16) he breaks over all restraint and says that since others (that is, his opponents) boast, he will also boast. Even at the risk of appearing to be a foolish boaster, he will speak freely about himself, for in his laborings and sufferings, as in the blessings that have fallen to him, he is not afraid to compare himself with others. He admits that it is "foolish" to do so, but they have compelled him to this; he has had to defend himself; the situation has demanded it, because the Corinthians themselves had not defended him as they should (xii. 11).

The fact that he had not received money from the Corinthians was used against him in a double way. It was said that that was a proof that he was not a genuine apostle; he had not the authority which belonged to the others (xi. 7). And on the other hand, it was said that he had had some deep purpose in this. He had not indeed taken their money, but that was a part of a plan by which he was going to get a much larger sum from them. The motive that had controlled him in this was not pure, as he had said; it was a shrewd, crafty policy, meant to deceive them. He had done this only that when the time came he might easily succeed in his nefarious purpose. Undoubtedly all this had reference to the collection which he was causing to be made in all his churches. It was a plausible charge, for how could they know whether Paul really delivered all the money that was passed over to him? Paul was wise enough to see that such charges were likely to be made, and had forestalled them by arranging that every congregation that sent money should also send a delegate with it, to see that their contribution reached its destined place. In the whole matter of the contribution he had asked the churches to appoint some one to travel with him, " one whose praise in the gospel is known throughout all the churches, that he might help in the collection and management of the money; for he had determined to make it impossible that any one should blame him and charge him with dishonesty in money matters. So we find several " messengers of the churches " with him, a part of whose duty it was to see that the money reached its destination (viii. 16-24). This throws a strong side light on the character of Paul.

They further said that he was not the equal of the apostles; he was not a genuine apostle; his gospel was false; he handled the word of God deceitfully, and his conduct was full of guile (xi. 5, iv. 2).

His defense is given with some bitterness, for he does not hesitate to pronounce a curse on them and all others who differ from him in his conception of the gospel (xi. 4). He calls them false apostles, deceitful workers, ministers of Satan claiming to be apostles of Christ (xi. 13–15).

His refutation of these charges is his success and the history of his life. The Corinthians ought to know that he is an apostle, for they had received the gospel through him. He surely did not need letters of introduction and recommendation to them! It could not be necessary for others to write to them that Paul was an apostle! They themselves were his letters, the proof of his apostleship, since it was through him that they had believed. His work among them had been eminently successful. He had not been behind even the very chiefest of the apostles. All the signs of an apostle had been wrought among them. Let not the Corinthians think that they had been converted through the efforts of a second-class apostle, for the same signs and wonders and mighty works had been performed among them as in other places. They were in no respect inferior to other congregations. "And yet there is one point in which you are inferior to others; I was not a burden to you; I did not receive any money from you, as other missionaries received from their converts. Forgive me this wrong!" (xii. 12–13). Such keen irony must have made them wince.

All his missionary life is also a proof of his apostleship, for he has suffered more than any one else for the cause of Christ. This accounts for the fact that there are so many personal reminiscences in this letter. He wishes to remind them of his life and all the opposition that he has endured. Unfortunately the charge of boastfulness oppressed him, and he could not speak freely of himself for fear that they would only laugh at him and regard what he said as proof of his boasting spirit. In spite of this, however, the letter is largely taken up with himself. He felt this, and at the end said, "I know that you are thinking that I am boasting all the time and excusing myself, and I admit it; but it is that I may strengthen your confidence in me and that you may be able to use this about me in arguments with those who oppose me and deny my apostleship." The whole letter is an apology, a defense of himself. Read such passages as iv., vi. 1–10, and xi. 22, if you would get an impression of the burden that he daily bore, and the dangers that hourly beset him. Much of the letter is taken up with himself and his work, but it was the only way to defend himself. But it is not written in the spirit of boasting. On the contrary, it is wrung from him with great anguish and pain.

Paul kept the promise which he had made to visit them soon. From Acts xx. 2 we learn that he spent some time in Macedonia. It is possible that he went further into the interior, and even reached the borders of Illyricum; for in Romans xv. 19 he says that he had preached the gospel even unto Illyricum. This must have taken place either at this time or during his first stay in Macedonia.

He reached Corinth in the autumn of 57, where

he spent three months. From here he wrote his letter to the Romans. The character of this letter is determined by the fact that neither Paul nor any of his immediate helpers had been in Rome. He was not acquainted with them and hence could not write a personal letter. It lacks the warm personal coloring of his other letters, for this can come only from intimate acquaintance. The letter is the ripest expression of Paul's views about the relation of the gospel to the law. In the struggle against the Judaizers he had developed his arguments and become perfectly clear about his doctrine. The letter is an attempt to outgeneral the Judaizers, and win the Roman church to his views before the Judaizers should enter the field. He determined to lay his gospel before them by letter, since he could not go in person. He first shows that the Jew through the teaching of the law, and the Gentile through the teaching of his conscience, must feel that they are sinners before God. It is impossible to earn salvation. The only way to obtain it is to believe God's word, and accept it as his free gift through Jesus Christ.

He excuses himself for not having come to them; it has ever been his desire to visit them, but thus far it has been impossible. For the present he must go to Jerusalem, but he expects then to go to Spain and will stop in Rome on his way.

After spending three months in Corinth he set out for Jerusalem in company with the various representatives of the churches in charge of the contribution. Because of the plot of the Jews he could not go by sea, but returned through Macedonia, and sailed from there just after the Passover. The account of the journey is exact and detailed, for it is taken from the diary of one of the company. The movements of the various members of the company are described as only an eye-witness could describe them.

The journey was a rapid one, for Paul wished to be in Jerusalem by Pentecost. On this account he could not visit Ephesus, but sent for the principal members of the church to meet him at Miletus, a port lying some miles to the southwest. After comforting and warning them, he continued his journey. The two chapters in which this is described are full of the most interesting details, which could have been given only by an eye-witness. The journey was in many respects a sad one for Paul. "Coming events cast their shadow before," and everywhere Paul was warned that dangers awaited him at Jerusalem. Even before he left Corinth he had been conscious that the Jews and Jewish Christians in Palestine would do all in their power to destroy him. All along the way prophets raised warning voices, forbidding him " through the Spirit " to enter Jerusalem. In every city the Holy Spirit testified that bonds and afflictions were in store for him there. But he was not to be disturbed by these things. Nothing can more clearly show how bitter was the hatred of the Jews and Jewish Christians to Paul, than the fact that everywhere the opinion prevailed that he could not safely venture into Jerusalem. At Caesarea they were the guests of Philip the Evangelist, also one of the seven, whose four daughters were prophetesses.

From here they took up their luggage and went up to Jerusalem in company with some of the Christians from Caesarea, and one of the early converts, Mnason of Cyprus, with whom they were to lodge in Jerusalem.

The very next day Paul with his companions visited James and the principal members of the church, and told of his labors among the Gentiles. With this they were well pleased, but they could not assure Paul that it would be so acceptable to all as it was to them. They called his attention to the fact that there were many thousands of believing Jews, but they were still zealous for the law. And these were informed that Paul had been teaching the Jews to disregard the law, and were consequently very angry at him. In other words, *Paul was in danger from the Christians in Jerusalem* as well as from the unbelieving Jews. It was impossible that they should not learn of Paul's arrival; it was necessary, therefore, to take such measures as would prevent their doing any violence to him. There were four men at hand who had a vow upon them, and Paul was asked to join them in this and show his fidelity to the law by paying the costs which attended the completion of the vow. It seems strange that a man who had written the letters to the Galatians, the Corinthians, and the Romans could have seen his way clear to take part in this matter, but the author of the Acts tells us that he did. It looks to us very much like deception on his part, but undoubtedly he felt that it was entirely in accordance with his principle, to become all things to all men that he might win some to Christ. Or shall we say that it is impossible that Paul should have engaged in such questionable conduct, and therefore the author of the Acts has not given us a correct account of this occurrence? It must be noted that the Christians here appear in the temple, which is still the centre of their religious life. They are still Jews, and have not separated themselves from those who refuse to accept Jesus as the Messiah.

CHAPTER VIII.

THE LAST YEARS OF PAUL.

While in Ephesus the plots of the Jews had caused him much trouble and suffering, and although he had left that city he could not escape their hostility. It was some Jews from Ephesus that caused his arrest. When they saw him in the temple they gathered a mob, seized Paul, and were about to make an end of him, when the captain of the Roman troops, stationed at Jerusalem, rescued him. He was taking him into the castle as a prisoner, to find out what the charges against him were, when, to his surprise, Paul spoke to him in Greek. He had thought that he was a certain Egyptian who not long before this had gathered together a band of four thousand Sicarii, or daggermen. These were most bitter opponents of everything that was Roman. They carried short daggers concealed under their robes, and managed to stab their enemies while they were surrounded by crowds, so that they could not be detected. Four thousand of these were brought together, and with them the Egyptian leader attempted to overthrow the Roman government. In the battle which followed they were nearly all slain, but the leader escaped. The governor thought he had captured this leader in the person of Paul. But when quiet was restored, Paul began to speak to the crowds, most of whom knew nothing of the cause of the disturbance. They listened till he began to tell them that he had been sent to preach to the Gentiles, when his voice was drowned by their shouts demanding his death. The captain ordered him to be scourged, in order to compel him to confess, when Paul informed him that he was a Roman citizen.

His trial was set for the next day before the Sanhedrin. In the midst of the trial Paul discovered that there were both Sadducees and Pharisees in the council, and very shrewdly set them against each other by declaring that the whole question was simply in regard to the resurrection of the dead. By this means he introduced strife among his opponents, and so escaped. The strife about him waged so warmly, however, that the captain feared he would be torn in pieces, so he took him back to the castle. Because of a plot to assassinate him the captain sent him to Cæsarea to the governor, Felix, and told his accusers they should appear before him with their charges. After five days the high priest and some of the elders came to Cæsarea, bringing with them an orator, or as we would say, a lawyer, to plead their case. This orator, Tertullus, began his speech with words of flattery for the proconsul, for then as now the principal effort was not to get at the truth in the trials, but to win the jury. In this case it was the good will of the proconsul that was to be won, and both parties had only good words for Felix. But Felix was won by neither party. He put off the decision until Lysias, the captain at Jerusalem, should come. In the mean time he kept Paul in safety, allowing him to see his friends and receive their care and attention. His conduct shows that he had some conscience, but no character. At times he listened to the gospel from Paul's lips, but was never quite ready to believe. At other times he was willing to favor the Jews, or at least unwilling to displease them, so he kept Paul a prisoner. Again, his cupidity showed itself, for he hoped that he might get a part of the contribution which Paul had brought up to Jerusalem.

In the account of all this it is very strange that not a word is said about any effort on the part of James and the Christians in Jerusalem to deliver Paul. They do not appear in any way as his defenders or even as his friends.

For two years he was kept in prison. It must have come as a much-needed vacation, for the years of restless activity and suffering had almost worn him out. In the spring of 60 Felix was succeeded by Festus, who, on his arrival at Palestine, at once went up to Jerusalem. The Jews laid another plot against the life of Paul, but Festus ordered them to appear before him in Cæsarea, if they had any charges to make against him. They came, charging him with being a transgressor of their laws and a political offender against Rome. He was said to be speaking against Cæsar by setting up another king, Jesus. It was very necessary for Festus, who had just come into the country, to get the good-will of the Jews. So he was willing to favor them. He was about to give Paul up to be judged by them according to their laws. Paul knew that that of course meant death, so he now at last made use of his right of Roman citizenship and appealed to Cæsar; that is, he claimed the right to appear in person before the Emperor Nero to be tried by him. That was the only way to escape. Festus was willing to sacrifice him to gain the good-will of the Jews. His only hope was in Nero. Besides, he had long been looking longingly toward Rome, and even though a prisoner he felt that he could yet accomplish something there, and he hoped, too, that he would thereby be freed from the plots of the Jews.

In the days of his residence at Cæsarea, Festus was visited by Agrippa II., King of Iturea, Batanea, and Abilene (50–100 A. D.), who came to congratulate him on his accession to the high office. He was accompanied by his wife, who was also his sister. They came in great pomp, and were received with honor. During their stay Festus remembered that he had a strange prisoner, and thought to add to the festivities of the occasion by making a show of Paul. The case was a puzzling one, for he could not understand the moral earnestness of Paul or the animosity of the Jews.

Paul was brought before them and was told that he might speak for himself.

True to his character Paul began with the most polite and deferential forms of address. Again he told the story of his life, and grew eloquent as he spoke of his Master. But Festus was unmoved. He saw in Paul only an old man whose head was addled by long disputing about trifling questions concerning the law. In the midst of Paul's address he called out "Paul, Paul, you are crazy," and attempted thus to end the interview. Paul knew that Festus was a Roman, but he hoped he might have had better success with Agrippa, who was a Jew. So he turned to him with an appealing question: "I am not mad, most excellent Festus; but speak forth words of truth and soberness. For the king knoweth of these things, unto whom also I speak freely: for I am persuaded that none of these things is hidden from him; for this hath not been done in a corner. King Agrippa, believest thou the prophets? I know that thou believest." But Agrippa was in the presence of a Roman who was ridiculing Paul and had no sympathy for either Judaism or Christianity. He did not wish to expose himself to the same ridicule, so he gave an evasive answer, "You think you can make me a Christian with little argument;" that is, "you think it will be an easy matter to convince me." The language is non-committal and ambiguous. Their meaning depends altogether on how the words were spoken. Seeing that the opportunity for further speech was gone, Paul called out: "I wish that all men, whether with little or great difficulty, were brought to be Christians as I am." But remembering that he was in chains, he quickly added in a half-playful way, "except that I would not wish to see them in bonds as I am."

Agrippa expressed it as his opinion that Paul might have been set free, but since he had appealed to Cæsar, to Cæsar he must go. The details of the voyage are given by one who saw them. It is described with some fullness and accuracy, and much of our knowledge of the technical terms of ancient navigation is derived from this description. The voyage was begun in the autumn of 60, but so late that the sea was already dangerous. The storms overtook them and they were shipwrecked on the isle of Melita, which is the famous Malta of the middle ages. After spending three months there they again sailed, and safely reached Puteoli near Naples. Here there were Christians who cared for Paul in every way possible during his brief stay there. Soon he began the long journey on foot to Rome. Some of the Christian brethren in the city had been informed of his coming and went out to meet him. At the forum of Appius, forty-three miles from Rome, a company of Christians cheered him with a warm welcome, and at the Three Taverns, ten miles nearer the city, still another little band came to meet him, and filled his heart with good courage. It was a great relief to him to find the Roman Christians so interested in him. For three years he had been in prison, and during all this time the Judaizers had been carrying on their missionary efforts. He did not know but that all his work was destroyed, and that they had triumphed everywhere. No wonder then that he thanked God and took courage when he found that the brethren in Rome were still so interested in and attached to him that they would come so far to meet and greet him.

True to his principle he first tried to reach the Jews. He asked many of them to come to see him and made known his gospel to them, but with only moderate success. From the nature of his case he was not housed with the criminals, but was put into the hands of the Prætorian Guard until such time as it should please Nero to listen to his appeal. For two years he waited, enjoying the privilege of living in a hired house where he could receive his friends and carry on the work so dear to his heart. But the prisoner's chain was upon him day and night. He was bound to soldiers who relieved each other at regular intervals.

There are four letters in the New Testament that are attributed to Paul, which were written during this period of imprisonment in Rome: the letters to the Ephesians, to the Philippians, to the Colossians, and to Philemon. But the genuineness of the letter to the Ephesians is questioned by a great many. For our purpose it matters very little whether it was written by Paul or not, for it lacks local color, and we learn almost nothing of the condition of the writer or of the church or churches to which it is addressed.

In i. 15 the people are praised for their general faithfulness in time of danger. In chapters iii. and iv. there are some references to the Gnostic ideas that were beginning to become prevalent. In several places there are indications that the author is a prisoner, and it is said that Tychicus will carry the letter to them and tell them more about his condition.

The letter to the Philippians is one of thanks. They had more than once given him money, and now that he was in prison they remembered that he would probably be in need and so sent one of their number, Epaphras, with another gift. Evidently Paul's condition seemed to Epaphras a hard one. In his zeal to do something for him he exposed himself and in consequence fell dangerously ill (ii. 25–30). This became known to the Philippians, and they now had a double trouble. Not only the situation of Paul weighed upon them. They feared also that their brother Epaphras would die. But he recovered, and as soon as he was able, Paul sent him back and with him this letter. It has been called a letter of rejoicing. But in spite of the many exhortations to rejoice, an infinite sadness and touching resignation pervade it. His situation was distressing, but with the true Christian spirit he was able to get comfort out of it all. He thanks them for their gift, but will not speak of his want, for he had learned (literally, " he had been initiated into the mystery ") to be content in any condition. He feels that life is hanging heavily upon him and wishes that it were ended. His heart is sore and bitter at the success of the Judaizing Christians, whom he calls "dogs, evil workers," and "enemies of the cross of Christ." Evidently that faction in the church was still laboring with great zeal to compel the Gentile Christians to observe the law, and that was a great trial to Paul.

Besides, there was strife in the church at Rome. There was rivalry between some of the leaders and Paul. They were envious of his popularity, and were preaching Christ in a factional spirit, trying to surpass him in success and popularity. It grieved him, but he felt no envy. It seemed to him that everything brought him trouble. But in one thing at least God had been merciful to him; he had spared the life of Epaphras that "I might not have sorrow upon sorrow." And he desires them to rejoice, that he may have a share in their gladness, and so be less sorrowful. He bids others rejoice. He declares that he himself is rejoicing, but it is clear that he was almost overwhelmed by sorrows and difficulties. There was almost nothing in his situation to cheer and gladden him.

The letter to the Colossians is interesting, and at the same time difficult, because of the references to the Gnosticism of the day, which was beginning to appear in the churches. This was a philosophical system of theology. It undertook to explain and define God, creation, sin, and redemption. It was at the same time a philosophy, a theology, and a religion. God was regarded as an infinite, indefinable, impassive spirit, so ethereal and fine that anything that is pure matter could have no connection with Him. He is the source of all good, while matter is the source and seat of all evil. The great question which troubled them was, How can God who is spirit and good create the world of matter, which is evil? An infinite chasm separates between God and matter. How can this be bridged? Can God be brought into connection with evil? How is creation possible? Their answer was as follows: God began the work of creation by producing from himself a creature only a little less fine in substance than himself, and from this He then caused another to emanate, which was still a little less fine, and from this another, and so on until He had at last produced one which was so coarse in substance that it could produce the world of matter. This one then created the world. These numerous creatures were all divided into certain ranks, and such names as "powers, and principalities, and thrones" were applied to the various grades. When people, who believed in these, heard of Christ and believed in him, one of the first questions which confronted them was, Where is Christ's place in this system? To what rank does he belong? These questions were much discussed and variously answered. It was to guard against error that Paul wrote to the Colossians that "Christ is the image of the invisible God, the firstborn of all creation; for in him were all things created in the heavens and upon the earth, things visible and things invisible, whether thrones, or dominions, or principalities, or powers; all things have been created in him and unto him, and he is before all things, and in him all things consist." Paul says, no matter how many angels and powers and the like you believe there are, Christ is above them all.

But people were at the same time seeking the way of redemption. They were asking how they might be delivered from evil and sin. From their idea of the character and seat of sin, the answer was not difficult. The flesh is the seat of sin; the spirit is sinless, except as it is contaminated by its contact with matter. To get rid of sin therefore one must get rid of one's body. To do so and live was of course impossible, but one must come just as near to this as possible. That led to asceticism. One must fast and scourge his body. "Touch not, taste not, handle not" was the common motto of many, as if they could be polluted by anything external. Paul has to remind them again that Christianity does not consist in such things, but rather in a heart right before God. This is the belief which made asceticism and monasticism possible. Unfortunately, Paul's rebuke of it was not able to destroy it. It has colored the belief and practice of the church ever since.

Philemon was a resident of Colossæ, who had been converted by Paul. Onesimus, his slave, after committing some crime, which is hinted at in the letter, ran away and went to Rome as the place where he could most easily escape detection. In some way he had been brought into contact with Paul, from whom he heard the gospel. After having brought him to a belief in Jesus, Paul sent him back to his former master with this letter. It is a charming one, which shows that Paul was truly human and not above making a pun. Onesimus means "profitable," and Paul easily makes a play on the word. It is as if he had written "Thy servant Profitable, who was formerly Unprofitable, but now Profitable to thee and to me." Paul says he would have been glad to keep Onesimus, since he needed the services of some one, but he felt it would have been presuming on the generosity of Philemon. According to the law a master could inflict whatever punishment he chose on a runaway slave. But Paul makes great demands for friendship's sake. He begs Philemon to receive him as he would himself; not as a runaway slave, but as a beloved brother. He also promises to make good whatever Philemon has lost through Onesimus. There is nothing said about freeing the slave, but he is to be treated as a brother.

This is in accordance with what Paul elsewhere says of slavery.[1] Nothing else would have more quickly put all the upper classes in opposition to Christianity than the announcement that it demanded that all slaves should be set free. Not

---

[1] 1 Cor. vii. 20, 21; Col. iv. 1; 1 Tim. i. 2, and elsewhere.

only Paul, but also all the writers of the New Testament saw this great danger. When in Corinth the slaves began to agitate the question of freedom, Paul wrote them that even if they had the opportunity to become free they should rather remain slaves, since before God they were free. But he marked out lines of conduct for both master and slave which would have reduced the evils of slavery to a minimum. It was all-important that the true character of Christianity should be known. It changes society, not by violent upheavals and revolutions, not by clearing away all the existing relations and introducing new ones made to order, but by changing the hearts of men. No change of the physical or social conditions of men will make them better. The change must work from within outward. Christianity was meant to sanctify all relations and positions in life by filling the heart with Christian love and love to God.

Although in prison, Paul was surrounded by some of his helpers. He is sure that he is about to be set free. So great is his confidence of this that he asks Philemon to prepare him a lodging in Colossæ, for he intends to go, not to Spain, but to the East.

This brings us to the spring of the year 63. Paul was in prison, but he expected to be set free soon, and was intending to go to the East. His trial was not over, but he was sure that it would end in his favor. But did it? There are some who say that he was never set free, but that he suffered death at the hands of Nero. But it is more probable that he was not put to death at this time. His cause had progressed so favorably that he was confident that he would be set at liberty. It must be noted again that this was in the spring of 63, but the persecution under Nero did not take place till August of 64. Besides, the letter to Timothy and to Titus cannot easily be located unless Paul was released.[1] We conclude, then, that Paul was released in the spring of 63. It is impossible to follow him with any degree of certainty from this time on. It had been his desire and intention to go to Spain, but we are not sure that he did so. There are two witnesses to this journey which seem to make it very probable that he actually made it.

The first of these is the so-called first letter of Clement of Rome. In a somewhat rhetorical passage he reminds the Corinthians that Paul had taught the whole world and had gone to the "limit of the West." These words can hardly be understood to mean anything else than that Paul had gone to Spain, which was commonly called the "limit of the West." It would be very strange if a Roman should speak of Rome as the "limit" of the West.

The other witness is the so-called Muratorian fragment, which speaks of the departure of Paul

---

[1] These letters are seriously questioned in nearly every quarter to-day, but there are certain parts of them that are genuine beyond all doubt. Nearly all of even the most radical critics admit this.

from the city (Rome) for Spain. No other church writers of the first centuries give any proof of this journey, and some even make sport of it, but it is certainly made probable by the testimony of these two good witnesses.

From the letter to Titus we get very little information. It is said that Paul and Titus had been in Crete, where Titus had been left to do certain work. Paul himself was going to winter in Nicopolis, but there were so many cities of that name that it is impossible to say which one is meant.

From 1 Timothy we learn that Paul and Timothy had been in Ephesus, where Paul had left his companion and gone on to Macedonia, where he expects to remain only for a short time, and then will return again to Ephesus. We learn, too, that danger was threatening the Christians from the civil authorities. The rulers were disturbing them, but these were not to be cursed, but to be prayed for that the Christians might not be troubled by them. Reference is also made to the Gnostic ideas, and it is said that some were making gain out of Christianity, — swindlers, practicing on the credulity of the brethren.

When 2 Timothy was written Paul was a prisoner in Rome. From this letter the probable course of events may be made out as follows: from iv. 13 we learn that Paul had been in Troas, where he had left his winter cloak and some parchments. From what follows it is probable that this was on his way to Ephesus, where he had been arrested.

Alexander the coppersmith, of iv. 16, is to be identified with the Alexander of Acts xix. 33. Paul had been arrested and had had a trial, during which he was deserted by all his Christian friends. They had left him to his fate. This points to a different condition of affairs. It is now dangerous to confess Christianity or to be known as a friend of its great missionary. Paul was bound and treated as a malefactor because he was a Christian (ii. 9). Even Demas had not had the courage to remain with Paul. He had not become an apostate, but was afraid to face the danger of death. Crescens and Titus were gone, but we cannot tell whether Paul blames them or not. But Onesiphorus made a brilliant exception to the general cowardice in Ephesus. He had cared for Paul and done all he could for him, in spite of the dangers that threatened; all the rest might turn away and desert the once popular preacher, but Onesiphorus remained faithful. He even followed Paul to Rome and there sought through all the prisons till he found him and ministered to him there also.

Paul felt this desertion keenly. It is impossible not to feel the pathos of the words, "Only Luke is with me." He knows that his race is run. "Dying with Christ," which had so long been his favorite figure of speech, is about to become a reality. Of the end there can be little doubt. There is a strong and steady tradition that he was beheaded in Rome. In later times this was greatly embellished and added to, but there is no good reason for doubting the fact. Clement of Rome, in the letter to the Corinthians (about 96 A. D.), takes it for granted that Paul had suffered martyrdom in Rome. About 200 A. D. Caius declares that the tomb of Paul was to be seen on the Ostian Way, just outside of Rome. The testimony of several others might also be quoted.

The death of Paul ends for us the apostolic age. With this event we leave sure history for the uncertain and conflicting traditions, which have been made more doubtful by the doubts which careful and thoughtful as well as biased historians have cast upon them. It will be well, however, for the sake of completeness to add what is most probable in regard to the other disciples. They may be dismissed with a few words, because so little is known of them, and it is not the purpose of this book to discuss theories and suppositions.

Of nine of the twelve we have absolutely no authentic information, but a learned German professor has collected three large volumes of the stories that were told about them during the Middle Ages.

James, the brother of John, was slain by Herod in the year 44.

The life of Peter was one of progress. His development has already been indicated in what has been said of his relations to Paul and to the Judaizers. We can trace it in the narratives about his preaching to Cornelius, the Council at Jerusalem, his conduct at Antioch, and his preaching at Corinth.

There is good evidence that he also ended his life by martyrdom at Rome. In the Gospel of John (xxi. 18-23) Christ is said to have foretold his imprisonment, and the author of this gospel understood it to refer to his death. The account was written long after Peter's death, so we may be sure that this also agreed with the real history of his end. Clement of Rome also speaks of his martyrdom, and connects him with those who suffered death under Nero. Ignatius, the Chronicles of Phlegon, Papias, Dionysius of Corinth, Irenæus, Tertullian, and Caius, all of the second century, bear witness to the fact that Peter had been in Rome, and was in a peculiar way connected with the church there. Dogmatic reasons have caused many Protestant writers to declare that he was never in Rome. But the weight of testimony is against them, and it may be accepted as a well-founded fact that Peter suffered martyrdom in Rome, probably in the last years of Nero.

The course of the life of the Apostle John is veiled in obscurity. The tradition which has most for itself is to the effect that after the death of Peter and Paul he removed to Asia Minor and settled in Ephesus, where he died at a great age. He is said to have been at the head of the Christian churches of Asia Minor. About the year 96 it is said that he was banished to Patmos, and that he died two years later. Several stories about him have been preserved by the writers of the second and third centuries, some of them very beautiful

But this tradition of his residence in Ephesus is not without its difficulties. In the first place, Clement of Rome, in the year 96, wrote as if all the apostles were dead. It is very improbable that he would have been ignorant of the fact if John had been still alive. A still graver doubt is thrown on this tradition through the fact that Ignatius, who lived and wrote his seven letters between the years 107 and 140, makes no mention of John. He was at the time passing through Asia Minor, a prisoner on his way to Rome, and wrote letters to the Ephesians, to the Philadelphians, to the Smyrnæans, to the Magnesians, to the Trallians, to the Philippians, and to the Romans. He speaks of Peter and Paul, but never once of John. If John had lived in Ephesus and labored throughout Asia Minor, is not this silence very strange, especially since his death must have been quite recent? But it is impossible with the present state of our sources to know what the end of John was.

The fate of James, the brother of Christ, is described by Josephus. He says that about the year 62 the high priest and the Sadducee party in Jerusalem caused his death.

CHAPTER IX.

THE OPPOSITION TO CHRISTIANITY.

CHRISTIANITY had two foes, Judaism and heathenism. From the first, the Christian preaching was polemic and apologetic against the Jews. They had the same book. The difference was one of interpretation. But so far as we know there were no written apologies addressed to the Jews during this period. Such writings did not appear until in the second century. The Epistle to the Hebrews was polemic, and written to show that Christianity is in every way better than Judaism. It is a comparison of the two, but it is addressed, not to the Jews, but to Christians. The Revelation is, in certain particulars at least, bitterly hostile to the Jews, but it is not addressed to them.

In Palestine there was apparently no opposition for three or four years after the death of Christ. The explanation of this is to be found in the fact that, in spite of the rhetorical passages in the Acts, Christianity did not make any great noise for a while, and its adherents were very conservative. The first opposition of which we learn was in connection with the dispute and address of Stephen. His free criticism of the Mosaic worship brought the mob upon him, and not only he suffered death, but there was a general persecution of the Christians in Jerusalem, many of whom had to flee from the city. We have only hints as to what they suffered, but it is clear that the Jewish authorities were in earnest in their efforts to crush out the young and rising heresy. Saul, it is said, was "breathing slaughter," which may be taken as representative of the attitude of the Jews. According to Paul's words he imprisoned men and women, scourged them in the synagogues, and even went to foreign cities to carry on his work of persecution. When they were put to death, he rejoiced at their fate. Possibly the letter to the Hebrews is addressed to the Jewish Christians in Palestine. If that be the case, some of them had endured a great conflict of sufferings. They had been in bonds for the truth's sake, and many had been deprived of their possessions (x. 32–34). The death of James and the seizure of Peter are attributed to Herod, but the fact that these things pleased the Jews makes it not improbable that they had something to do with it.

In other countries their opposition was none the less bitter, although they were not always able to convert their hatred into action. No matter where Paul went, he was seldom free from their plots and violence. From Rev. ii. 9 and iii. 9 we learn that there was trouble there between the Christians and the Jews, who are called the synagogue of Satan, because they were trying to imprison the Christians.

The means which they used were various. Whenever they could they stirred up the mob as the surest way of accomplishing their purpose. References to this method of procedure are common, as in Acts xiv. 19, where it is said that the Jews from Antioch and Iconium persuaded the multitudes and stoned Paul and left him for dead.

In xvii. 6 the Jews of Thessalonica are said to have got a mob together to drive out Paul and Silas. Before the governors they also made charges against the Christians that they were traitors to the government and were preaching another king, Jesus. Sometimes they appealed to the authorities to stop the spread of the sect simply on religious grounds. They demanded that the Roman law protect and assist them in their efforts to compel the observance of the law.

In order to inflame the populace against the Christians they also spread abroad evil slanders concerning them and their meetings. Thus it was declared that in their nightly meetings under the cover of the darkness they practiced unnatural crimes, indulged their lust promiscuously, and even murdered children, whose flesh they ate and whose blood they drank. The early fathers say that all these stories originated with the Jews. The only trace of such things to be found in the New Testament is in Acts xx. 8. At Troas, where Paul preached late into the night, the author is careful to say that there were many lights in the room where they were gathered together. This sounds strange. What need was there of making such a statement? We would think it entirely unnecessary. It is probable that the author wished to guard against malicious slanders and evil surmisings, and so emphasized the fact that the room was well lighted, and hence there would be no possibility of practicing the evil deeds with which they were charged.

At Philippi and at Ephesus Paul and his companions were subjected to persecution and violence, because their work had cut off the gains of certain men or classes of men.[1]

The heathen writers of the first century took no notice of Christianity. They did not think it worth refuting, and they did not regard it as powerful enough to be dangerous to the state. Their silence is not strange, for most of the Christians belonged to the lower classes. Christianity was not a fashionable religion. As a movement it did not attract the attention of the educated. It built no great temples; it had no mysterious and imposing sacrifices or ritual. Besides, it came from the Jews. It was in fact

---

[1] The reader will easily recall the opposition with which Paul met at Damascus, Jerusalem, Antioch, and elsewhere, but if he wishes to get the full force of this, he should collect all the passages in the writings of the New Testament which refer to opposition or persecution. In this way he will get a good impression of the bitterness and violence to which the Christians were subject by the plots of the Jews. It is needless to say that since the Christians came into power with Constantine they have repaid the Jews with heavy interest.

regarded as a Jewish sect, and so its adherents were regarded with the same dislike and prejudices as the Jews. More than this, there were no Christian writers that appealed by their writings to the general public. They addressed no apologies to the heathen, and produced no polite literature that would challenge the attention of the educated world. Not one of the writings of the New Testament is addressed to the heathen. Christianity was for a long time propagated by the spoken, not by the written word.

But there were certain things about Christianity which made it impossible for the local Roman officers to let it go unnoticed. The government was very watchful against the nightly meetings of clubs and secret societies, for they were likely to be the hotbed of conspiracies. The character of their meetings made the Christians seem very like such a club, and hence their meetings might be interrupted and punished by the police at any time.

Eastern religions, except Judaism, were forbidden. So long as Christianity could pass as a Jewish sect, it was undisturbed, but when it became clearly differentiated from Judaism it became at the same time a proscribed religion, and to be a Christian was to be a criminal in the eyes of the law.

Another ground of persecution was found in the attitude of the Christians to the heathen temples and idols, their holy days and processions. Almost every neighborhood had its temple and god, which was regularly honored on fixed days by a great gathering, a feast, and a grand procession. Naturally, the Christians withdrew from these celebrations. Nothing could have been more offensive to their friends and neighbors, for their conduct seemed to be inviting the wrath and vengeance of the god. They attributed the breaking out of an epidemic disease, or the failure of the crops, drought, storms, or any calamity, to the anger of the gods, the cause of which was not far to seek: they were offended at the Christians who despised them and refused to pay them their proper honors. Such "atheists" must be brought to sacrifice, or be removed from the land. In consequence of this, the Christians in many places suffered violence at the hands of the infuriated mob that had taken it upon themselves to guard the honor of their gods and remove the cause of their anger.

The rise and rapid spread of the worship of the Emperor has already been spoken of. It had pervaded the life of the people to such an extent that it was the most common form of idolatry practiced in the empire. To refuse to sacrifice to the Emperor was to be guilty of both sacrilege and high treason, the punishment of which was death by beheading, burning, or by being thrown to the wild beasts in the arena. To refuse to sacrifice before his statue was to be guilty of sacrilege, because it showed a lack of respect for holy things; and it was treason, because it was an offense against the Emperor's majesty and a denial of his divine dignity.

It was here that the Jews showed their malignity, and found ample opportunity to vent their religious hatred under cover of the law. They early learned that the safest way was to inform the officers of the government of the presence of Christians. Their religious enmity was the moving cause, but in each case they made the charges which would be most effective and have greatest weight with the authorities. It is a significant fact that in almost all the accounts of martyrdoms in the second and third centuries there are Jews present, stirring up the people and urging on the punishment of the Christians.

The form of the trial was, for the Christians, a most unfortunate one. There was but one way to clear themselves of the charge, and that was by offering sacrifice before the statue of the Emperor or at the altar of some idol. In order to be set free they must defile their conscience and deny their God. They were not asked whether they were guilty of any crime, such as murder, fraud, or theft. It mattered not how pure their lives, how upright their conduct, simply to be a Christian was to be a criminal, and the only satisfactory evidence to the contrary could be furnished in but one way, by sacrificing to the gods and denying the name of Christ. Throughout the first three centuries there is one long protesting cry heard from the Christians against such unfair treatment. They urged that a crime could not consist in a name, and pointed to the gross injustice that was apparent in setting a thief or libertine free because he worshiped the gods and denied Christ, while the pure and upright were put to death, simply because they confessed the name of Christ.

There are many references in the book of Revelation to the worship of the Emperor and to those who had suffered martyrdom because of their refusal to take part in it. The oft-recurring expression "to worship the beast and his image" means to worship the Emperor and his statue. In ii. 13, it is said that Satan's throne is at Pergamum, an expression which refers to the great number of heathen temples there. Among them was one to the Roman Emperor, and Antipas had suffered martyrdom because he had refused to worship him. A careful study of the whole book will reveal the fact that nearly all the martyrs that are mentioned have suffered for this same cause. It will be seen, too, that the background of the book is not Rome and the persecution of Nero, but Asia Minor and the general attitude of the government to the Christians, which often caused local persecution and oppression.

Two Roman Emperors of the first century have covered themselves with lasting infamy by their treatment of the Christians. These are Nero (54–68) and Domitian (81–96).

The persecution by Nero is connected with the burning of Rome. On the night of the 18th of July, in the year 64, a fire broke out in the city and raged for six days and seven nights before it could be extinguished. But it soon broke out again in a new quarter of the city, and it was three days before it could be brought under control. About two thirds of the city were in ashes, the people were without shelter, and most of them could not even distinguish the place where their homes had once been. But worst of all, their beloved temples and favorite altars were swept away too. The common belief was that Nero had caused the city to be burned. This was strengthened by the fact that the second fire began in the house of one of his favorites. It must be said, however, that he himself was not in the city when the fire began. It is known that Nero had expressed a wish to rebuild Rome and to beautify it. The streets were crooked, narrow, and in many places unsightly. It was his ambition to make these straight, and, by entirely rebuilding the city, to have a good pretext for naming it after himself, "Neropolis." Besides, there was ground in various parts of the city which he wished to possess, but thus far it had been impossible for him to obtain it. But after the fire it is a well-known fact that he seized possessions in many places, a thing which was very easy, since all the landmarks were gone. At any rate, there was a strong belief that he had done the mischief, and the people were raging against him. It was necessary for him to have a scapegoat that he might be able to turn the suspicion and anger from himself.

Tacitus tells us that under these circumstances some Christians were seized and charged with the crime. Being put to the torture, they confessed that they were guilty, and gave the names of many of their fellow-Christians, who were seized and put to death with the most refined cruelty. Some of them were crucified. Others were sewed up in skins to resemble wild animals, and fierce hunting dogs were turned loose upon them. Others were covered with inflammable material, dipped in pitch, and elevated on poles to serve as torches to illuminate the garden of Nero in which races were held. Nero himself, in the dress of a charioteer, contended in the races.

The age of Nero was intensely realistic in art. On the stage, it often happened that the play ended literally with the death of the actors. For such characters, criminals were used. Many of the myths were dramatized and exhibited as "living pictures." Some of the Christians were used for this purpose also. Dirce, the enchantress, had used her arts on Antiope, but her two sons avenged their mother by tying Dirce to the horns of a wild bull and causing her to be dragged to death. This story of Dirce has been represented in plastic art in the famous group known as the Farnese Bull. This had been dramatized, and Christian girls and women were compelled to play the part of Dirce, being tied to the horns of the infuriated beasts and dashed to death as they rushed about the arena. Still others had to play the part of the daughters of Danaus. We do not know in just what form this myth had been dramatized, though it is not improbable that they were given over to the lust of men, possibly of the soldiers.

Such were the punishments, but how many suffered? We have no means of knowing. Both Tacitus and Clement, writing entirely independently of each other, say " a great multitude," but this is only a general expression, and does not help us to form an opinion of the exact number. To any humane man, even fifty such sufferers would seem a great multitude.

We must seek to discover why the Christians should be chosen as the scapegoat and the crime laid upon them. Suetonius says it was in part because they were given to a new and criminal superstition. That is, because they were addicted to a new Eastern religion, which was forbidden by the laws of Rome. Tacitus says that Nero charged them with the burning of Rome, but implies that the Romans did not believe them guilty, but that he merely took advantage of the fact that they were hated by the people, in order to turn the attention of the populace from himself. Their unpopularity may be attributed to two causes: first, they were hated because of the base deeds which they were thought to commit in their nightly meetings; and second, they were said to hate the whole human race, since they took the surest means to bring destruction upon it, by refusing to honor the gods and to perform the duties of good citizens.

But still we may ask the question, why did Nero select the Christians? Why not the Jews, for they also were unpopular. There are two possible explanations of this. The wife of Nero, Poppæa, was either a Jewess or a proselyte. She was the friend and advocate of the Jews at the court, and was surrounded by them. Through her influence Nero was also friendly to the Jews, and many of his favorites were of that nationality. When we consider the bitter hostility which the Jews had toward the Christians, it at once becomes very probable that the Jews at the court of Nero took this opportunity of involving the Christians of Rome in ruin. It would be easy for them to suggest to him that the language and belief of the Christians could easily be interpreted in such a way as to make it appear that they were probably the guilty ones, for they constantly spoke of the kingship of Jesus, and of his return to judgment, and of the destruction of the world by fire. Their words could be easily garbled and given a political coloring.

But it is possible that this was brought on them through the action of some faction in the Roman Church. For Clement of Rome says that the persecution was caused through "envy and strife," but the envy and strife of whom? Of the Jews, of the Judaizers, or of some faction among the Christians themselves? Only two years before this, Paul had written to the Philippians that some were preaching Christ "out of envy and strife." All these are possibilities. It is impossible to say which is the more probable.

There is still one question which we must ask about this persecution. Did it extend beyond Rome, or was it confined wholly to the city? There is not the least evidence to show that the Christians outside of Rome were troubled by it. There was no general edict against the Christians, and none were arrested except those of the city. The whole persecution was improvised. Nero neither knew about nor cared for Christianity, but he was suddenly brought into such a situation that it was necessary for him to find some one whom he could treat as guilty, and so turn the anger of the people from himself. It was simply the misfortune of the Christians that in some way his attention was turned to them, and they had to suffer. The state was not persecuting Christianity as such, but in an evil hour they were called on to suffer through the caprice and cruelty of the Emperor.

And yet the persecution did affect the standing of the Christians, at least in many provinces. It made it clear to all the local authorities that the Christians were not the favorites of the Emperor, and hence might be punished with impunity. It no doubt led to greater vigilance on the part of the officers of the state, and hence to many single arrests and executions. Through this, the situation of the Christians was made much less secure, and they were exposed as never before to petty annoyances and to the dangers of arrest. It was this change in the general situation and safety of the Christians that forms the background of the book of Revelation.

The persecution under Domitian was by no means a general one, and it is probable that only a few individuals were affected by it. The fate of Flavius Clemens and Domitilla has already been recounted. Eusebius, in his Chronicon, says that many Christians were put to death in the last years of his reign. Clement of Rome excuses the Roman Christians for not having written earlier to the Corinthians because of the sudden misfortunes and calamities that had befallen the congregation in quick succession. Domitian's cruelty was caused largely by the fact that he was in need of money. This led him to make use of spies and informers, whose business it was to hunt out all those who could be charged with any infraction of the laws, and bring them before the Emperor that he might invent some pretext for seizing their property. In this way, some Christians suffered rather because of his cruelty than because they were Christians. Yet it is possible that he also issued edicts aimed against both Christians and Jews, for Dion Cassius says that his successor, Nerva, when he came to the throne, pardoned those who had been condemned because of "impiety" (a common charge against the Christians), recalled those who had been banished, and forbade that any should be tried on the charge of "impiety," or for adopting the Jewish faith. This can only mean that he undid the action of Domitian, his predecessor, but it is not clear just what shape this action had taken.

The persecutions of the early Christians have

been greatly exaggerated for rhetorical as well as apologetical purposes, but enough has been said to show that their situation was far from a safe one. The real history of their sufferings has never yet been written by man. Only brief fragments of it have escaped the oblivion of the years, but even these fill us with a strange sadness and sympathy, and give us the desire to know all that they dared and suffered for their faith. It would show us the measure of their attachment to Jesus. But this will not be known till that great day when all hidden things shall be brought to light.

CHAPTER X.

AUTHORITIES, GOVERNMENT, AND WORSHIP.

We must begin with the fundamental fact that every Christian was thought to possess the Holy Spirit by virtue of his confession of his belief in Jesus as the Messiah. He received the Holy Spirit, which brought him into a direct and intimate relation with God. He received the spirit of adoption which enabled him to call God "Father," and address Him as a child would address its father. This filial relation and intercourse of the individual believer with God because of the possession of the Holy Spirit is one of the basal beliefs of the first Christians. The believer is said to walk in this spirit, to live in it, and to be controlled by it. Paul felt this truth perhaps most strongly of all the writers of the New Testament, and gave it its classical expression when he said, "I live no longer, but Christ lives in me."

Whatever natural means or ability the believer possessed were regarded as a gift, a Charisma, which must be used in some kind of service for his fellow-Christians. Paul often gave expression to this truth. In Romans xii. 4 ff. he says, "For even as we have many members in one body, and all the members have not the same office: so we, who are many, are one body in Christ, and severally members one of another. And having gifts differing according to the grace that was given to us, whether prophecy, let us prophesy according to the proportion of our faith; or ministry, let us give ourselves to our ministry; or he that teacheth, to his teaching; or he that exhorteth, to his exhorting: he that giveth, let him do it with liberality; he that ruleth, with diligence; he that sheweth mercy, with cheerfulness." Thus he regarded the ability to prophesy, to minister, to teach, to exhort, to give, to rule, to show mercy, as gifts of the Holy Spirit out of God's free grace. In similar language in his first letter to the Corinthians he tells us that there is but one spirit, but a great variety of gifts, as of wisdom, of knowledge, of faith, of healings, of prophecy, of speaking with tongues, of helps, of gifts, and so on indefinitely. Every believer was raised to the high position of a king and priest before God, for he was destined to reign with Him, and had access to his presence in prayer without the intervention of any man or class of men whose special prerogative it was to deal with holy things. Every one who has the Spirit has direct access to the Holy of Holies, to the throne of God himself. What need was there then that any one should be invested with a special authority? What room or place was there for the thought of a special inspiration which should give its possessor an absolute authority? If each one lives in direct communication with God, how can he admit that any man or book may have an authority for him? For himself he needed no external authority. This was the theory of the early Christians, but facts are more powerful than theories. The practical exigencies of the situation radically modified the workings of their theory.

The belief in the Messiahship of Jesus carried with it one duty. It was the duty of the individual as well as of the whole body of believers to convince both Jews and heathen that Jesus was the Messiah sent of God. To do this, they had to have authorities and proofs. Besides that, in a few years after the death of Christ, ideas and beliefs were entertained by many in the church which seemed to others to be hostile to Christianity and subversive of its principles. To refute these and protect the church there was need of authorities.

The first of these was the Old Testament. Everywhere in the New Testament we find the Old quoted, and used as an authority which must not be questioned. Jesus himself used it as an authority, in spite of the fact that he at times quoted it only to replace its teachings by his own. He did not hesitate to set over against "It is written," "But I say unto you."[1] He recognized its authority in a general way, but put above it the higher truth which he felt himself to possess.

---

[1] In Matthew, ch. v., Jesus uses the formula, "It has been said," or, "Ye have heard that it was said," to introduce quotations from the Old Testament, and then offers his teaching in opposition to it.

Paul declared that the whole Old Dispensation with all its authorities were forever done away and were no longer binding on the Christians, and yet he drew from the Old Testament collateral evidence for many of his teachings and principles. Above all, he used it to prove that Jesus was the promised Messiah, by showing that many of its prophecies and much of its language applied to him. But it is safe to say that the Old Testament would not have held its place on the same plane of authority with the words of Jesus but for the fact that it was so constantly used to prove his Messiahship.

The highest authority of all was Jesus, as represented by his words and deeds. To be able to quote one of his sayings was to settle any point of dispute or uncertainty. Our Gospels are meant to be simply collections of his sayings, though they do not contain them all. When writing to the Corinthians, Paul was often able to quote some saying of Christ bearing on the question in hand, and in such a case there was no further appeal. The matter was decided once for all. He was careful to distinguish between the words of Jesus and his own opinions, and never thought of putting them on the same plane of authority. When he could not quote a saying of Christ he sometimes said, " I give you my opinion ; I believe I have the Spirit, but you may take it for what it is worth." Besides the words of Jesus, his deeds, or better, perhaps, his life, were regarded as an authority.

His was the normal life which was to be imitated by his followers. His deeds, such as the institution of the Lord's Supper, his death and resurrection, were regarded as having an absolute value, and must not in any way be questioned or denied.

Besides these, there were prophetical and apocalyptic writings in circulation, which have found a place in neither the Old nor the New Testament, which were, however, regarded as authoritative. It was taken for granted that these possessed authority, for they were believed to be the product of the Holy Spirit.[1] Several of these enjoyed a high reputation and were for a long time read in the churches, and almost succeeded in maintaining a place in the canon of the New Testament.

A certain authority was thought to attach to all those whose calling it was to speak for the edification of believers. There were apostles, prophets, and teachers, whose gift it was to speak the word of the Lord. Not only the Twelve, but all who were sent to bear the message of the gospel, were called apostles. This is made clear from 1 Corinthians xii. 28, and from the "Teachings of the Twelve Apostles" (chapters 11–13), which throws much light on the passage in Corinthians in which apostles, prophets, and teachers are mentioned. These did not belong to the local band of Christians, but as the prophets of old were sent to the whole Jewish nation, so these apostles, prophets, and teachers were given to the whole church, and

---

[1] Two such writings are quoted in the Epistle of Jude.

therefore they were regarded as having a certain degree of authority.

Lastly, it was felt that those who had first embraced Christianity, those who were "presbyters," that is, "seniors" in years and experience, were entitled to a regard and reverence which amounted to admitting them to the rank of authorities.

These were the various authorities of the early Christians, all of which can be easily discovered from the writings of the New Testament. They were not coördinated or arranged in the proper order, nor was the amount of authority attaching to each determined. They did not form a legal and dogmatically fixed canon of authority. They simply had authority from the very nature of the case, and not because of any dogmatic considerations. They had authority because of their character, which appealed to the common sense of those who believed. The pupil has some reverence for his teacher. The convert looks up to the missionary who instructed him in the way of life. The man who knows much about any subject is an authority for those who are ignorant about it. These things are so naturally, not because of any dogmatic reasons. Above all, the modern dogmatic idea of inspiration must not be applied to them. For such a thing is entirely foreign to the writers of the New Testament.

The possession of the Spirit did not confer an absolutely infallible authority. Two men might "have the Spirit," and the one refuse to obey the other. This is clear from the account in Acts concerning Paul's last journey to Jerusalem. In every city the Holy Spirit testified unto him that bonds and afflictions awaited him there. *The disciples said to him through the Holy Spirit that he should not set foot in Jerusalem,* but he heeded them not, because he felt that he also had the Spirit.

From this point of view it is not difficult to say a few plain words about the government of the early church. It was a gift and not an office. Just as there were those who had the gift of exhortation or of prophecy, so there were those who had the gift of ruling. Just as some set themselves to minister to the poor, so others took it upon themselves to manage the affairs of the congregation. All who served in any capacity were "deacons," for deacon means one who serves or helps. It was many years before this word hardened into the technical meaning of "a church officer inferior to the presbyters, whose duty it was to look after the temporal affairs of the congregation." In the New Testament, διάκονος occurs about thirty times. Only three times is it translated "deacon;" in every other case it is translated "minister" or "servant." The verb διακονέω is used about thirty-eight times. Only twice is it translated "to serve as a deacon." In every other case it is translated by some general expression, the fundamental meaning of which is that of service of some kind. It can be successfully maintained that διάκονος is never used in the New Testament as the technical name of a church officer. Even in Philippians i. and 1 Timothy iii. 8, 12, the passages yield a meaning much better and more in accordance with the known facts if it is translated by some general word such as helper. The meaning of the passages in 1 Timothy is that not every one is to be allowed to engage freely in the work and affairs of the congregation, because some were doing so from unworthy motives. All helpers must be of a certain moral character. There is as yet no office in the congregations, but they are beginning to have some supervision over the exercise of the "gifts" of their members. It is at most a step toward the formation of an office. To be a "deacon" was still to be simply a voluntary helper, serving the congregation in whatever way one was best fitted to serve.

In the same way "presbyter" meant simply elder or an old man. This is the prevailing use of the word. Thus in writing to Timothy (1 Tim. v. 1, 17) Paul advises him not to rebuke an old man, but because of his age to exhort him as a father; the old men who rule well, that is, the old men who through their counsels wisely manage the affairs of the congregation, should have double honor, the honor that attaches to age and the honor that is due them for their good freewill services. It is true in all countries, and especially in the East, that the old men are regarded with honor and their opinions allowed great weight. But age does not constitute an office. It was only natural that the younger should be in subjection to the older (1 Peter v. 6), but this was not because the latter held an office, but because of the honor and dignity that naturally attached to age. There are many indications in the literature of the first and second centuries that the elders were the old men of the congregation, who by courtesy, because of their age, had the right to a voice in the management of its affairs, and not because they were officers duly elected and claiming the authority by a divine right. It lies beyond the purpose of this book to trace the gradual transformation of this honor and of the "gift" of ruling into an office. It was a process which began in the apostolic age, but was not completed till long after.

What we know about the church at Antioch and the church at Corinth ought to be decisive as to this point. At Antioch it was not the bishops or presbyters and deacons that managed the congregation, but there were prophets and teachers, through whom the Holy Spirit spoke. The most minute study of the letters to the Corinthians fails to discover any reference to a church officer of any kind. Everything was in the hands of the whole church, and its affairs were managed and its work done, not by officers, but by the freewill exercises of the various gifts of all its members.

But officers were soon found to be necessary, and a government of some kind had to be invented, for societies cannot exist without some kind of government. There was, however, no uniform system of government, but each congregation governed itself as it chose. The history of this and the growth of the episcopal form of government belong to the following period.[1]

The worship of the Christians was free and unrestrained, and there was no fixed ritual that was everywhere followed. Worship was not separated from their daily life and common duties. The worship of God was not confined to set times, but pervaded their lives. The performance of every duty was an act of worship, because done in his name. They came together as often as possible. The social and religious were so harmoniously blended that they could not be separated. There was certainly no more than the faintest resemblance between their gatherings and what we call divine services. One thing, however, soon became fixed in their gatherings. A portion of the Old Testament was read. They early began to read the letters of the apostles and of others, that were in circulation. Reference is made to this custom of public reading in the book of Revelation i. 3, in the words, "Blessed is he that *readeth* and they that *hear* the words of the prophecy."

Nearly all our information of the services is derived from the first letter of Paul to the Corinthians. From this it is evident that there was the

---

[1] On the subject of the government of the early church, the reader is referred to the work of Hatch, *The Organization of the Early Christian Churches.*

greatest liberty of speech. One has a psalm, another has a teaching, another a revelation, another a tongue, another an interpretation, and another a prophecy. The custom of taking up a collection for the poor was early introduced.

Baptism " in the name of Christ " soon became universal, if it was not so from the very beginning. It will be remembered that Apollos was a Christian, but knew nothing of Christian baptism, and Paul found a few persons in Ephesus who likewise believed in Christ, but knew nothing of baptism in his name. There is nothing to show that there was any importance attached to the person who performed the rite. Peter simply commanded the household of Cornelius to be baptized. Paul did not regard baptizing as an essential part of his apostleship. The Lord sent him not to baptize, but to preach. It was looked upon rather as the confession of Christ by the one who was baptized. It was his act, not something performed on him. It symbolized a change of character and consequent admission into the kingdom of the Messiah. It seems to have taken place not in the meetings of the Christians, but whenever any one was convinced of the genuineness of the claims of Jesus. Even the disciples did not at this time use the " Trinitarian " formula in baptizing, but used only the " name of the Christ." There is not the slightest trace of the use of the Trinitarian formula in baptizing in the apostolical writings. Everywhere it is spoken of as baptism " into," " in," or "upon the name of the Christ" (Acts ii. 38, viii. 16, x. 48, xix. 5; Rom. vi. 3; 1 Cor. xii. 13; Gal. iii. 27). The Gospel of Matthew, which contains the Trinitarian formula for baptism, was not written till some time after the death of Paul.

The celebration of the Lord's Supper was also not connected with formal worship, for, as we understand that, such a thing did not exist for a long time. They followed the example of Christ, and broke the bread and partook of the cup at the close of the daily meal. When they came together it was their custom to partake of a meal in common, and the eucharist naturally came at the close of this brotherhood meal. As to its meaning, we find two different ideas attached to it. The one of these is represented in John's Gospel and reappears in the "Teaching of the Twelve Apostles." This is the idea of life. Just as the bread sustained the physical life, so they believed that they might feed on Christ, that in them eternal life might be produced. The other idea is found in Paul's first letter to the Corinthians, and is that of the forgiveness of sins. The bread and cup were visible reminders to them of the fact that the body of their Lord had been broken and his blood shed for their sins. They remembered that he had made himself an offering for sin.

It is difficult to speak of their life and worship, because we attach such different meanings to the words which we are compelled to use. Such a distinction as is now made between secular and religious was impossible for them. Christianity filled their lives. It was a new relation to God. They felt themselves to be his children, and all their time and strength belonged to Him. It could not be said that some of their acts were more holy than others, for all were produced out of that new principle of life which had been implanted within them, and all that they did was done in the spirit and name of the Christ. Every duty, however menial, was sacred, and its performance an act of worship.

CONCLUSION.

It remains to point out briefly some of the lines of future development, the beginnings of which are to be found within our period. Some of these have been already indicated. The Judaizers and the strict Jewish Christians had made Paul's life a burden to him during his last years. They were zealous for the law, and did all they could to destroy his work among the Gentiles. References to them in Paul's latest letters show that they were still at work, even after he had been long in prison. But when, in the middle of the second century, we again get a clear view of things, we find that they have deserted the field. The mass of Jewish Christians had given up the law and were united with the Gentile Christians. What had brought about this change? In one word, the fall of Jerusalem.

From about the year 60 A. D. the Jews of Palestine were in a state of perpetual revolt. The pages of Josephus give us some idea of the factions, the bands of robbers and murderers and the false Messiahs, that kept Palestine in a fearful state of anarchy. For several years Rome was slow to take up the work, but when she began it was done with characteristic Roman thoroughness. The siege of Jerusalem was long and bloody. The city was conquered literally by inches. The walls which were destroyed by day were rebuilt by the Jews in the night. A bitter famine increased the horrors of the siege. Finally, in August of 70, the temple was taken and burned. Josephus says this was contrary to the orders of Titus, but he was friendly to the Romans, and wished to appease the Jews. Sulpicius Severus in the fourth century says that Titus had ordered it to be burned, and his sources of information were the lost books of Tacitus.

Undoubtedly a large majority of Jewish Christians were patriotic, and fought for their law and their homes and shared the fate of the vanquished. Tradition says that they had been warned to flee from the city, and that they went to the little city of Pella, beyond the Jordan; but there is nothing to show that the thousands that believed and were zealous for the law deserted their country in the hour of danger.

The fall of Jerusalem was of the greatest importance to the Christian church, and its influence on the course of events can hardly be overestimated. It was believed that Jesus had foretold its destruction, and it was regarded as a fulfillment of his prophecy. The destruction of the temple caused the ritualistic worship to cease. It confirmed the belief of the Christians that the temple's mission was ended. It was an expression of God's judgment on the Jews. Their power as a nation was completely gone, their temple destroyed, their holy place defiled. God had deserted his unfaithful people. He would have no more of their sacrifices. He had utterly cast them off, and so set his seal of approval on the mission to the Gentiles. It opened the eyes of the Jewish Christians to these facts. They were forced to interpret it as an expression of God's anger with his people. This weakened their adherence to the law, and led them to associate with the Gentile Christians, and finally brought about their complete union. It separated the Jews and the Jewish Christians, for the latter were persuaded that it was because of the sins of the former that all this had taken place. There was now no longer the danger that a narrow Judaistic type of Christianity would prevail. It relieved Christianity from the pressure which the Jewish Christians had put upon it. It was left free to develop itself along more liberal lines.

But not all the Jewish Christians gave up the law. Small bands of them still held to it and refused to associate with the Gentile brethren, but from this time Jewish Christianity became less and less important. It ceased to have any influence on the life and progress of the church. The few congregations that kept the law shut themselves off from the rest of the Christian world, and, by refusing to mingle with other Christians, lost their only opportunity to influence the development of the church. They were in an uncomfortable position, for the Jews cursed them and the Christians regarded them as heretics. They were pressed on both sides. Several of the church fathers warned against them, and various nicknames were applied to them. They did little to increase their numbers and make converts. They did not follow the first Judaizers in their strenuous missionary efforts. We know of but one writer, Symmachus, who represented their beliefs in his writings. The future was not theirs. It belonged to the Gentile Christians whom they despised. After dragging out a pinched, miserable existence for a few centuries they disappeared, leaving no trace of their influence.

The Jewish Christians who united with the Gentiles carried with them their personality, their many Jewish conceptions and hopes, and helped to mould the church. Many of the phenomena of the history of the church in the next centuries are to be explained by this fact. They helped keep the writings of the Old Testament on the same plane with those of the New, and infuse a spirit of legalism into the church, which is not yet wholly cast out. How much influence they had on the development of the priesthood it is difficult to say. But there is evidence to show that the writings of the Old Testament contributed their share to it.

It has been shown that "gifts" (Charismata) occupied a prominent place in the thought and life of the Christians. The church was a brotherhood, without a fixed government. Its members served, each with his peculiar gifts. But as their numbers increased, some kind of government was necessary. The logic of events created offices. Sometimes committees were formed for special purposes. Sometimes offices were created in imitation of the societies and clubs that existed throughout the empire. These offices tended to become permanent, and their incumbent's power greatly increased. In this way they encroached on those whose services had been voluntary. Opposition arose between those who had gifts and those who had offices. Of these "charismatic" persons, the prophets were the last to yield. This struggle culminated in the movement known as Montanism at the end of the second century. The outcome could not be doubtful. The officers were organized, the prophets were only so many individuals. Regularly appointed officers of the church came to control everything. There was no longer room for the free exercise of gifts of any kind. The clergy dominated everything. The offices and the honors were theirs. Obedience to them became the test of church membership.

Jesus had said that religion is a matter of the heart. He taught not a theology but a religion. But those who came to believe in him brought with them their ignorance and many of their superstitions. Their false conceptions of things were not corrected by a belief in the Messiahship of Jesus. They brought with them their metaphysical speculations. They came into Christianity with all their intellectual possessions. The problem which pressed upon them was, How can Greek culture of the day be harmonized and united with the teachings of Jesus? The difficulty which the Gnostics of Colossæ had in fitting Jesus into their speculative system was but the first of a long series that were to trouble the church and vex its peace. It was inevitable that there should be a fusion of Christianity with the philosophy and superstition of the Greeks, in which the former was sure to suffer and lose much of its simplicity. The religion of Jesus became corrupted, his religion was replaced by a philosophy.

The Sermon on the Mount, with his lofty ethics, was eventually replaced by the Athanasian Creed, with its subtle metaphysics. The oneness of Jesus with the Father in love, will, and purpose was replaced by a oneness in substance. The religious and ethical greatness of Jesus was obscured by the speculation about his metaphysical relations to God.[1]

[1] See Hatch, *The Influence of Greek Ideas upon Christianity.*

APPENDIX.

THE CHRONOLOGY OF THE PERIOD.

It must be emphasized at the outset that it is impossible to fix all the dates of this period with certainty. What is here offered is given as a *working* basis. It is not claimed that they are absolutely correct.

Just a word as to the process of determining them. It seems to be certain that Porcius Festus became Procurator and reached Cæsarea (Acts xxv. 1) in the spring of the year 60 A. D. Paul had already been two years a prisoner (Acts xxiv. 27). That fixes his arrest in Jerusalem in the year 58 (Acts xxi. 27 ff.). After Festus came, Paul appealed at once to Cæsar, and probably set sail for Rome in the autumn of 60, but because of shipwreck did not reach his destination until the spring of 61. These dates may be regarded as well established. From the various indications given in Paul's letters and in the Acts, combinations must be made, and we reckon from these dates backward and forward.

	A. D.
The Crucifixion	30
Stephen's death	33–34
Conversion of Paul	34–35
His labors in Arabia, his return to Damascus, his visit in Jerusalem, and his return to Tarsus	34–45 until about 38

His labors in Tarsus, *about*	38–43
The conversion of Cornelius	40
The founding of the first church among the Gentiles at Antioch	42
Barnabas brought Paul from Tarsus to Antioch, *about*	43
James the brother of John slain by Herod Agrippa II., who was king over Judæa, Galilee, Perea, etc., 41–44, *Easter*	44
Paul made the journey described in Acts xiii.–xiv., *about*	44–51
The so-called council at Jerusalem	50 or 51
Paul's missionary journey through Asia Minor, Macedonia, Greece, and his residence in Corinth; the so-called second Missionary Journey, *about*	50–54
His residence in Ephesus, the so-called third missionary journey	54–58
Paul's arrest in Jerusalem . at Pentecost	58
Felix, Procurator	52–60
Porcius Festus, Procurator	60–62
Paul imprisoned in Cæsarea	58–60
In the autumn Paul sailed for Rome, which he reached in the following spring	60
His imprisonment in Rome	61–62 or 63
Probably set free, his journey to Spain? His return to the East	62–63
His second arrest in Ephesus, sent to Rome where he suffered martyrdom. Probably Peter also suffered martyrdom about the same time in Rome	64–65 or later
The death of James, the brother of Jesus, in Jerusalem	62
The Fall of Jerusalem	70

The death of John is said to have occurred about 98. Practically for us the apostolic age ends with the death of Paul, for we have no certain information about the whereabouts or labors of any of the other apostles.

INDEX OF TEXTS.

GENESIS.
ix. 6 ....151 *n*

LEVITICUS.
iii. 17............151 *n*
vii. 26............151 *n*
xvii. 10-24 ......151 *n*
xviii.............150

ISAIAH.
liii. 10............108

MATTHEW.
v..................290
v. 17..............133

JOHN.
iv. 37 *f*..........56
xxi. 18-23........271

ACTS.
i.-viii. 3..........62 *n*
i. 15..............64
ii.................71 *ff*
ii. 38.............299
ii. 42-47..........87 *n*
ii. 44, 45..........77
iv. 32.............77
iv. 34, 35.........77
iv. 36, 37.........120
v. 12-16..........87 *n*
v. 42.............87 *n*
vi. 9............95, 102
vii. 58............102
viii..............18 *n*
viii. 1-4..........37
viii. 16..........299
ix................104 *f*
ix. 1-30..........89 *n*
ix. 19.............37
ix. 23-25.........111
ix. 31.............38
ix. 32 *ff*.........46
x. 2..............32 *n*
x. 26-30..........113
x. 48.............299
xi.-xii. 25.......62 *n*
xi. 19-21..........41
xi. 20.............53
xi. 25............115
xi. 26.............44
xi. 27-30.........116
xii. 12............78
xii. 17............46
xii. 25...........116
xiii..............18 *n*
xiii.-xiv..50, 89 *n*, 177 *ff*
xiii. 1 *ff*........44
xiii. 9............90
xiii. 50..........32 *n*
xiv. 19...........275
xv.............128, 142 *ff*
xv. 1.............141
xv. 23............114
xv. 27............149
xv. 29............150
xv. 36-xxi. 26....159 *n*
xvi. 6............163
xvi. 14...........32 *n*
xvi. 20, 21.......169
xvi. 37...........92 *n*
xvii. 6........51, 275
xvii. 28 ....14, 93
xviii. 5..........176
xix...............18 *n*
xix. 1............193
xix. 5............299
xix. 22...........213
xix. 27...........197
xix. 29...........197
xix. 31...........195
xix. 33...........269
xix. 39...........197
xx. 2.............249
xx. 8.............275
xx. 31............195
xxi. 17-26........157 *n*
xxi. 20........47, 129
xxi. 27 *ff*......307
xxii..............104 *f*
xxii. 28..........92 *n*
xxiii. 5...........98
xxiv. 27..........307
xxvi...........104 *f*, 307
xxvi. 10...........96
xxvi. 16..........119

ROMANS.
Rom...............159 *n*
i. 16..............149
ii. 6-16..........137
ii. 26-29.........137
ii. 28-30.........139
iii. 1 *ff*........148
vi. 3.............299
xii. 4 *ff*........288
xvi..............48 *f*, 50
xvi. 3, 4.........200
xvi. 10............50
xxi. 10, 11........57
xvi. 14............50

1 CORINTHIANS.
1 Cor....157, 159 *n*, 214 *ff*
i. 11..............213
i. 26..............54
iii. 18............219
iv. 1..............119
iv. 7..............213
iv. 8-13..........221
v.................222
v. 5..............212
vi. 1-11..........222
vi. 12............223
vii...............223 *ff*
vii. 8.............96
vii. 20, 21.......265 *n*
vii. 21...........228
viii..............226 *ff*
viii. 13..........150
ix................229 *ff*
ix. 1.............104
ix. 5........47, 50, 161
ix. 18-23.........157 *n*
xi. 17-34.........231
xii.-xiv..........232
xii. 13...........299
xii. 28...........292
xiii..............235 *f*
xiii. 4-7.........236
xiv. 2.........75, 79

xiv. 5...............75	xi. 13–15..........248	iv. 1..............265 n
xiv. 14..............75	xi. 16.............246	iv. 11................91
xiv. 27..............75	xi. 22.............249	
xiv. 34.............229	xi. 22–29..........101	**1 THESSALONIANS.**
xv.................236 ff	xi. 25........123, 170	1 Thess.....159 n, 175 ff
xv. 3–8..............68	xi. 32, 33.....111 bis	ii. 2...............170
xv. 6................64	xii. 7..............97	iii. 2..............180
xv. 8...............104	xii. 11............246	iv. 11.............78 n
xv. 32..............200	xii. 12, 13........248	
xv. 33..............93	xii. 14............239	**2 THESSALONIANS.**
xxi................238	xii. 20, 21........245	2 Thess.....159 n, 178 ff
xvi. 9.............199	xiii. 1............239	ii. 2..............179
xvi. 10, 11....213, 214	xiii. 2........240, 245	iii. 10, 11.........78
xvi. 12............222		iii. 17........98, 179
	GALATIANS.	
2 CORINTHIANS.	Gal........159 n, 205 ff	**1 TIMOTHY.**
2 Cor.............159 n	i. 15–17...........110	1 Tim............267 f
i. 8–10............199	i. 17..............104	i. 2..............265
i. 14..............243	i. 22, 23..........115	iii. 8–12..........295
i. 15–17...........240	ii..........130, 145, 152	v. 1–17...........295
i. 17..............245	ii. 1, 2...........143	
ii. 1..............239	ii. 7..............45	**2 TIMOTHY.**
ii. 4..............241	ii. 9..............147	2 Tim............267 f
ii. 5–11...........245	ii. 11 ff..........151	ii. 9.............269
ii. 12.............242	ii. 11–21........157 n	iv. 13............268
ii. 17.............244	iii. 19............94	iv. 16............269
iii. 1.........244, 246	iii. 27............299	
iv..............201, 249	iv. 4...............2	**TITUS.**
iv. 2..............247	iv. 13..........163 bis	Titus.............267
v. 12..............246	iv. 13 ff...........98	i. 12..............93
v. 13..............245	iv. 21–31........140 n	
v. 16...............95	iv. 29.............94	**PHILEMON.**
vi.................201	v. 12..............211	vs. 9........92, 265 ff
vi. 1–10...........249	vi. 11..........99, 210	
vi. 3–10...........102		**HEBREWS.**
vi. 11–13......242, 243	**EPHESIANS.**	x. 25..............18
vii. 2–4...........243	Eph...............260	x. 32–34..........274
vii. 2–16..........242	i. 15..............261	
vii. 8–11..........241	iii.–iv............260	**1 PETER.**
viii...............244		v. 6..............296
viii. 1–5..........172	**PHILIPPIANS.**	v. 12.............162
viii. 16–22........243	i. 1..............295	
viii. 24...........243	i. 12–26..........100	**JUDE.**
x..................201	i. 13..............56	Jude.............292 n
x. 1–10............245	ii. 25–30..........261	
x. 7...............244	iii. 3............140 n	**REVELATION.**
x. 18..............246	iv. 16........171, 172	i. 3..............297
xi. 4..............247		ii. 9.............274
xi. 5..............247	**COLOSSIANS.**	ii. 13............280
xi. 6..............245	Col..............262 f	iii. 9............274
xi. 7..............246	ii. 16............139	

www.ingramcontent.com/pod-product-compliance
Lightning Source LLC
Chambersburg PA
CBHW030015240426
43672CB00007B/961